17

SEA FISHING

The Wash to Thames Estuary

Also in this series

SEA FISHING IN CORNWALL

SEA FISHING IN SOUTH DEVON

SEA FISHING IN NORTH DEVON AND SOMERSET

SEA FISHING IN DORSET

SEA FISHING IN HAMPSHIRE AND THE ISLE OF WIGHT

SEA FISHING HUMBER TO THE TWEED

SEA FISHING IN KENT

SEA FISHING NORTH WALES AND ANGLESEY

SEA FISHING IN SUSSEX

A COMPLETE GUIDE TO SEA FISHING

SEA FISHING

The Wash to Thames Estuary

IAN GILLESPIE

ERNEST BENN LIMITED · LONDON

First published Ernest Benn Limited 1969
Bouverie House . 154 Fleet Street . London . EC4

© IAN GILLESPIE 1969

Printed in Great Britain

510-21521-1
510-21552-4 *Paperback*

FOR NINA

Foreword

IT IS NOT the purpose of this book to teach anyone how to catch fish, though the novice or the relative newcomer to sea angling may pick up a few useful hints which will help him if he should fish in the area which has been covered. Primarily, the object is to put before the reader in logical order, the basic information which will enable him as a visitor to this part of the East Coast, to go to the right place, know what he is likely to find there as far as species, sport and conditions are concerned, and to choose tackle which should give satisfactory results.

From Skegness in Lincolnshire down to Canvey Island on the north side of the Thames Estuary is something well over two hundred coastal miles. No angler alive is conversant with all the sea fishing to be had along this tremendous stretch of coastline, and in compiling this book I have leaned heavily on the knowledge of many anglers who fish in various localities. I have added what knowledge I have gained during my own activities during the last twenty years spent fishing in East Anglia.

Without the willingness and co-operation which I have encountered, the book would have been quite impossible to write. It says a great deal for the spirit of the sport of sea angling in this part of the world that from the start I have met with nothing but a genuine desire on the part of sea anglers, boatmen, bait diggers, tackle dealers and club officials, to help as much as possible in ensuring that the information contained in the book is useful and reliable. I think that I can assure the reader that nothing of great significance has been omitted and that, apart from the inevitable changes which must occur concerning boatmen, club officials, etc., the details given are accurate.

I would like to offer my sincere and grateful thanks for a great deal of help from the following anglers:—

Colin Hill (Skegness), Dick Reynolds (Hunstanton), Miss Barbara Hall (King's Lynn), Vic Edge (Holbeach), Deryk Story (Kings Lynn), E. Waller, E. R. Waller and S. Jarvis (Cley), Terry Pearce and Tim Riches (Cromer), Sam Hook and Ted Bean (Lowestoft), Frank Moore (Great Yarmouth), H. Land (Southwold), George Linsell (Aldeburgh), Rex Sheppard and Sandy Powell (Felixstowe), G. A. Osborne (Frinton), Mike Lilley and Peter Nunn (Clacton), Tony Gregory, Arthur Ord and Ian MacGregor (Brightlingsea), P. Littlewood, L. M. Larkins and A. J. Shelley (Southend), M. J. Ashby (Canvey Island) and Peter Collins of *Angling Times*.

I would in addition like to offer particular thanks to my good friends Fred Williams of Great Yarmouth, John Sait of Brightlingsea and Bill Roberts of Southend, all of whom have done far more to make the book a useful one than I could ever have reasonably requested them to do.

As time passes and situations alter, revision will be necessary. It is also possible that minor corrections or omissions will need to be dealt with, and I hope that anyone who feels that he can help in this direction will contact me, care of the Publishers, so that anglers in this area may be served more adequately.

Ian Gillespie, January 1969.

Contents

Foreword   page 5

Introduction   11

Skegness   15

The Wash and District   21

Cley to East Runton   31

Cromer and District   37

Great Yarmouth and Gorleston   57

Suffolk Coast   67

Essex Coast   95

Thames Estuary   117

INDEX   127

Charts

1 Coastline: The Wash to Thames Estuary   page 10

2 Skegness   16

3 Hunstanton   20

4 Cromer   38

5 Yarmouth and Gorleston   58

6 Lowestoft   66

7 Southwold   74

8 Orfordness   81

9 Shingle Street to Felixstowe   84

10 Harwich Harbour   94

11 Essex Estuaries   102

12 Southend and Canvey Island   118

Illustrations

[between pages 64 and 65]

1 The biggest cod ever caught on rod and line from a boat off the British Isles

2 Crab, lug and squid baits

3 One man—many cod

4 Hazards of a crowded pier

5 Roy Leeder with bass of 14¾lb taken off Felixstowe

6 The 'Old Style'

7 'And the New'

8 Fred Williams with Norfolk beach-caught thornbacks

9 Small East Coast dinghy off Felixstowe

10 A 12lb thornback comes to the gaff

11 An average East Coast cod

12 Mr. A. Hoolhouse with plaice of nearly 4lb from Cromer Pier

LINCS

Skegness

Gibralter Pt.

Boston

THE WASH

Holme
Thornham
Brancaster
Scolt Head
Hunstanton

Holkham

Wells

Stiffkey

Blakeney Point

Cley
Saltbouse
Kelling
Weybourne
Sheringham
Beeston Regis
W. Runton
E. Runton
Cromer
Overstrand
Trimingham
Mundesley
Walcott
Ossend
Happisboro
Cart Gap
Eccles
Sea Palling
Waxham
Horsey
Somerton

Kings Lynn

NORFOLK

NORWICH

R. HOLBURG

Winterton
Hemsby
Newport
Scratby
California
Caister
Yarmouth
Gorleston
Hopton
Corton
Lowestoft
Pakefield
Kessingland
Benacre
Covehithe

Southwold
Walberswick
Dunwich

Minsmere
Sizewell
Thorpeness

Aldeburgh

SUFFOLK

IPSWICH

Orford

Orfordness

Shingle Street
East Lane

Bawdsey

Felixstowe Ferry

Shotley

Felixstowe

Landguard Point
Harwich
Dovercourt

COLCHESTER

The Naze
Walton

Frinton

Holland

Clacton

Mersea
Island

Jaywick

CHELMSFORD

R. Blackwater

Sales Point

Dengie Flats

FLOODING TIDE

ESSEX

Ray Sand

R. Crouch

Foulness Point

CHART No.1
COASTLINE
COVERED

Southend

LONDON

Canvey

Shoeburyness

Thorpe Bay

RIVER THAMES

Introduction

THE SEA ANGLER who talks of the East Coast talks, in the same
breath, of the superb cod fishing for which the area, particularly
parts covered by this book, is justly famous. For twenty years, Sam
Hook's 32lb cod, taken from the Claremont Pier in Lowestoft,
was unchallenged as the British record. Only the tremendous increase in the amount of sea fishing practised in the country as a
whole has resulted in the fish having since been bettered by a
handful of others. The record is now held by a Welsh fish, of
44½lbs, but early in 1968, Tony Marsh, of Ipswich in Suffolk, came
very near to dislodging it with a magnificent 43lb cod, taken from
his dinghy two miles off Felixstowe, in Suffolk.

Big fish apart, however, the cod fishing is still outstanding. Many
an angler has taken home a hundredweight of smaller fish at the
end of a day, and to them the achievement was possibly more
satisfying than one monster might have been. As an angler, the
reader may have no ambition either to break the record, or to
catch more fish than he knows what to do with. It says much for
our cod fishing, however, that if either fancy takes him, he can fish
nowhere else in the British Isles with greater hopes of succeeding.

Though the cod fishing colours the whole outlook on this coast,
other species are well worth fishing for. Huge tope can be found
in the Wash, and off certain beaches, autumn whiting fishing is
often superb, thornback rays fall in large numbers to beach
anglers of the calibre of Fred Williams, of Yarmouth, and the
25-year-old British record held by the late F. C. Borley with his
18lb 2oz bass, taken from the beach at Felixstowe, is not as un-
typical a catch for the area as many anglers would have others
believe. Tremendous catches of dabs, plaice and flounders are
frequently taken, there is good sport to be had at times with
mackerel and mullet, and a host of other species are caught from
time to time. If the cod, the whiting, the flatfish and the thornback
ray are the mainstays of our sea fishing, the lack of basic variety
is compensated for partly by the promise of the unexpected, and
wholly by the quality of the fishing which is provided by these
dominant species.

BEACH FISHING

GENERALLY speaking, but certainly with some exceptions, the beach
angler fishing in these areas will find himself operating with gear
which, in other parts of the country, would be regarded as heavy.
The tidal flow dictates the choice, on many occasions, of spiked
grip leads up to and sometimes over six ounces. The long casting

which can sometimes be a definite advantage, needs a powerful rod and a correspondingly strong line. The modern hollow glass beachcaster, lines of around 20 to 30lb, the multiplier or fixed spool reel, these are an efficient and wise choice. Anglers fish with cane rods and centre-pin reels, and they do catch fish, but, inevitably, the more modern tackle is gradually becoming standard equipment.

Lighter gear can be used in places and at some stages of the tide, of course. Spinning tackle, float fishing gear and much lighter beach outfits than that already described, all these have higher applications. The fact remains, however, that any angler who intends to fish anything like a reasonable amount of the coastline covered in this book will find the heavier outfit the most useful one.

Terminal tackle varies a great deal, as is natural when so many newcomers to the sport are constantly solving the problems of catching fish to their own satisfaction. In general, however, the nylon paternoster, with one, two or three booms, is widely used. Another common arrangement, used frequently by good cod and thornback fishermen, is the single blood loop or boom, tied above the lead, with a snood varying in length from just a short dropper to a long flowing trace. Almost without exception, the successful fisherman restricts himself to one hook when he is after heavier fish. A ten pound cod or thornback in a powerful tide is quite enough of a handful on its own. The prospect of hooking two at once and landing neither does not appeal to the experienced local.

The lugworm accounts for ninety per cent of the cod and whiting taken, and for a very large proportion of other fish, too. For tope, thornbacks, bass and whiting, fish strips are widely used, and other baits will be mentioned from time to time when their use is important.

Lugworm is still, at the moment, in reasonably good supply, though the quality varies, especially in the warmer months. There are large stretches of beach where no bait is diggable, and a very flourishing trade in worms is carried on by tackle shops up and down the coast. Parts of north Norfolk do have an extensive natural colony of worms, and tens of thousands are dug and sold daily. Costs have increased since the closure of many small railway stations, and the perceptible decline in the number of worms to be found by the diggers has also caused prices to rise. Current cost of the ' blow ' lug, which is the most common variety, varies from nine shillings per 100 when bought direct from the diggers, to twelve shillings when collected from the retail sources. In the height of the cod season, therefore, when a successful day's fishing will exhaust upwards of 100 worms per rod, bait is an expensive item. Almost without exception, the angler who cannot dig his own must order and pay for it well in advance. Dealers with highly perishable worms on order do not take kindly to anglers who order without paying, then turn over in bed when the alarm goes off, or the weather is dirty. Sources of bait supply are mentioned from time to time as each area is covered.

BOAT FISHING

TAKEN as a whole, and with the exception of the Southend area, boat fishing is not as organised, as far as the visiting angler is concerned, as it is in other well known fishing centres. In many places the dangerous tides and the treacherous sandbanks which run almost entirely along this coast, keep charter boat fishing to a minimum. Not many owners will leave even dinghies in the hands of visitors they do not know well, and this is understandable. As things are at the moment, the boatmen who do operate are regularly booked at weekends by anglers of long acquaintance, who charter boats for a season at a time in order to be sure of places. Often enough, the boatmen have other jobs during the week, and some are frankly not interested in getting more trade. In places, however, the visitor can arrange to be taken out, and information is given where this service is available. In the absence of concrete information, the visiting angler should contact one of the reliable and knowledgeable tackle dealers in the area, and will often be put in touch with boatmen with whom personal arrangements can be made.

SMALL BOATS

THE visitor can, of course, trail a smaller craft with him. In places, this is a sensible idea. and can lead to excellent fishing. It must never be forgotten, however, that the weather on this coast can, even in apparently settled spells in summer, change for the worse very rapidly. All the river mouths are treacherous in one way or another, open beaches are very prone to produce a wicked surf if wind direction becomes unfavourable, and in addition there are many sandbars lying just offshore which may prove very difficult, if not impossible, to negotiate if tide and wind combine unfavourably. The reader must therefore take very seriously these general warnings, and he will find these supplemented more specifically in the coverage of each area. Having digested all that, he must not fail to seek advice from locals on every occasion. Many fatal accidents have occurred here, and it is certain that many more will occur.

As far as fishing results are concerned, there is no doubt that the boat angler often finds himself in a world apart compared with the beach angler. A twelve-foot dinghy is in many cases a passport to successes which would not be achieved from the beach. There are days when a beach rod accounts for nothing, and a boat angler just a few hundred yards offshore enjoys tremendous sport. The shallow inshore water, the holiday crowds and the natural caution of the fish in daylight hours throughout the year are often detrimental to beach results. The boat angler will on the other hand, be singularly unfortunate to draw a complete blank on any day of the year, and when things go well his catches can be literally staggering.

Almost without exception, boat fishing is carried out with the boat at anchor. Very strong tides, snaggy bottom and the evidence gained by experience make fishing at anchor the wisest course. There are times when drift fishing might be more productive, but the visitor will find very few locals who are conversant, or even concerned, with this style of boat fishing. A long anchor rope is therefore essential, and a tripped anchor a wise precaution.

Space precludes the setting out of lengthy and helpful advice concerning the handling of small boats in these waters. There is a great deal to bear in mind whenever and wherever this type of fishing is carried out. I sincerely hope that no one reading this book will be impressed enough with the fishing available to disregard the basic fact that boat fishing is, and always will be, seventy per cent seamanship, and thirty per cent angling. Since this book concerns fishing, I should like to make a point of stressing that it does not set out to give more than basic advice to the angler who has never taken out his own boat before. The East Coast is certainly not the place to learn by trial and error, and this book is not the one to rely upon for comprehensive instruction concerning small boat handling.

It is true to say that boat fishing produces catches similar to beach fishing, only more so. With the exception of consistent tope fishing and the best of the mackerel, there are no species which are approachable only by boat. I leave each angler to decide for himself whether the satisfaction of beach fishing is enough, or whether he seeks the increased quantity, but not necessarily better quality, available from a boat. Personally, though I do a lot of boat fishing, I would not miss those dark November nights when the cod are running, the surf pounds up on to freezing shingle, and a roaring gale sweeps along my lonely beach, for any boat fishing in the world.

PIER FISHING

THERE are several piers in this area which, at various times of the year, provide excellent sport. Rather than generalise at this stage, I have dealt with each in the locality concerned, and the reader will find all relevant information there. The only point to be emphasised now is that all piers have one thing in common, in that they attract the general public as well as the angler. The sea angler's image is, I am convinced, formed by the public from what is observed on our piers. Judging by the amount of litter, stale bait, crushed crabs and slaughtered, immature fish which I have seen from time to time, the image cannot at the moment be as good as it might be. I hope that the reader will do all he can to improve it.

1. Skegness

SKEGNESS. (CHART NO. 2)

TIDES: $+4\frac{1}{2}$hrs High Water London Bridge.

Fishing from this popular Lincolnshire seaside resort is possible from beach, boat and pier. The tides dominate the attitude of the sea angler because the distance between high and low water marks is considerable, and this can lead to danger for the beach man as well as hard work pulling a boat over the sand after a day's fishing. Tides are strong, with the flood a little more powerful than the ebb, with the result that the advancing water comes in quickly over a shallow sandy beach. Patches of mud or shingle occur in places, particularly in the Ingoldmells area, and to the south near Gibralter Point the beach is flanked by low sand hills, which occur again to the north of Skegness.

BEACH FISHING. Reference here is made to the eight miles of fishing available from Chapel Point and south to Gibralter Point. Fishing is usually carried out on the flood, since few fish appear to feed on the rapidly retreating ebb. At high water itself and as an exception to the rule, Chapel Point, Ingoldmells Point and Mastins Corner offer fishing for an hour or so of the ebb as well.

Chapel Point is generally considered to be the most productive area, but the incoming tide can here cut the unwary angler off from the beach, as it can at the other Points mentioned, and in the whole area south of Jackson's Corner and down to Gibralter Point. The general procedure when in danger of being cut off is to walk to the north as quickly as possible.

The beaches are fairly clear of snags beyond the low water mark, though crab pots and pegged beach lines may be encountered. The angler intending to fish up to high water should note the positions of breakwaters, wooden groynes, and the remains of old sea defences which are frequently uncovered by changing sea conditions. The breakwaters and groynes extend from Chapel St. Leonards south to Winthorpe.

Dabs are taken throughout the year, but the best of these occur between September and January, with October and November being particularly good. The autumn months give good sport, too, with the ever-present flounder. Spring fish are normally in poor condition after spawning. Before Christmas, cod to 10lb are taken, but afterwards the average size drops, though the fish remain until April. There are always small whiting to be caught in the autumn, and occasionally a run of better fish to 2lb or so occurs in October,

15

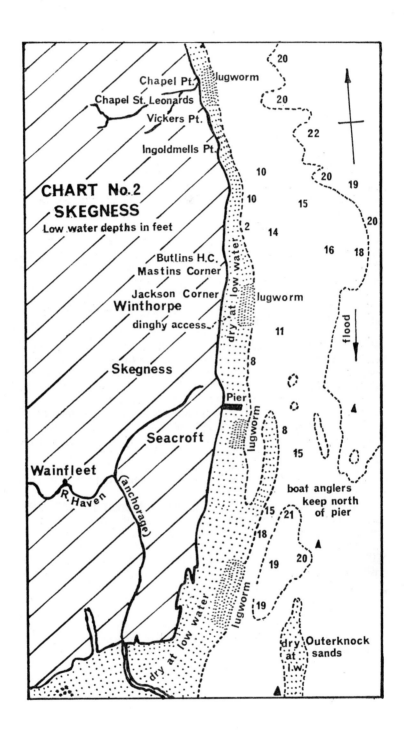

CHART No. 2
SKEGNESS
Low water depths in feet

and again in March. Beach-caught thornbacks are normally small, as are tope and bass, but the occasional good fish does turn up. Other species include eels in the summer months, a sprinkling of soles, bull huss, spurdog, coalfish and sea trout.

Winds always play an important part in the angler's activity, and here the locals favour a moderate S. West or West for good results. Anything over force three or so between North and East makes beach conditions very difficult, though a South-East wind appears to liven up flounders.

SKEGNESS PIER. With the exception of silver eels, everything taken from the local beaches is taken more frequently and to better size from this pier, which is over half a mile long. In addition, certain species such as mackerel, big tope and the occasional brill and conger come within reach, which they almost never do inland. The pier is open from Whitsun through to October between 9 a.m. and 10 p.m. daily. From October to May it opens on *weekdays only,* and from 9 a.m. to 4.30 p.m. During this period, and occasionally at other times of the year, the local pier angling club obtain permission to have the pier available ' out of hours '. An extra charge of 1s per rod is then added to the normal daily ticket of 1s.

Three hours either side of high water is the most productive time on the pier, and the fishing area is free of all but the occasional temporary snag, carried in by fierce tides. A drop net is available, owned by the local Pier Angling Club.

In spite of the fact that boat fishing is carried on at Skegness, many of the local records have been established on the pier. These include tope (female 44lb, male 31lb), cod (14$\frac{1}{4}$lb), dab (1lb 3$\frac{1}{2}$oz), flounder (1lb 12$\frac{1}{4}$oz), thornback (17lb) and brill (1lb 3oz). It is certain that flounder over 2lb and whiting over 3lb have also been caught, but for various reasons they do not appear on the local lists.

The autumn dab fishing here can be excellent, with thirty fish per rod not unknown. In March 1968, over 300 fish to a pound or so were taken in one day by forty anglers. June and July are productive for thornbacks, and July and August often sees shoals of mackerel off the pier. During the first week of September, 1961, eight tope to around the 30lb mark were taken, and many more fish lost.

BOAT FISHING. Since there are no boats available for hire, the only course open to the visitor is to bring his own, or fish as a guest with a local boat owner. There is no harbour at Skegness, but at Gibralter Point there is an anchorage for boats up to thirty feet, in the River Haven. This tidal water is navigable for only two hours either side of high water on spring tides, so that departure and return times are critical.

B

Dinghies can be launched from the beach in many places, but the angler must remember that a long pull, often over soft sand, will be necessary if he returns at or near low water. Returning at high water also has its hazards, since groynes, breakwaters, etc. may be covered. General access is difficult for boats during the holiday season, but reliable access points are at Trunch Lane (between Chapel and Ingoldmells Points), Jackson's Corner (Skegness Sailing Club base), and Winthorpe Avenue. Others are at Chapel St. Leonards, Vickers Point, Ingoldmells Point and North Shore Road (north end of Skegness).

Owing to the intricate and dangerous nature of the sandbanks, the visiting boat angler is not advised to fish south of the pier. North of the pier the depth is fairly uniform, and there are no hazards. With low-lying land masses behind, winds from any direction at all can create launching and boating difficulties if they are at all strong. In addition to using his common sense, the visitor may obtain useful information and current conditions from H.M. Coastguard, Tel: Skegness 3075.

In addition to all the local beach and pier species, the boat angler has the best chance of consistent sport with mackerel, thornbacks and tope. Mr. K. Daubney and Mr. A. E. Hewison, both local anglers, took ten tope totalling 163lb in a three hour session in 1963. Boat anglers fishing off Chapel St. Leonards have taken many thornbacks to 18lb, and in 1966 Mr. Hewison broke the male tope record, previously held with a pier fish, by boating a tope of 35lb.

BAIT. The vast majority of local species are taken on lugworm or herring strip. Lug can be dug from several places at low water, and local supplies are available if ordered in advance. Lug accounts for all species apart from tope and thornback, which are taken on fish baits, and it is herring strip which appears to tempt the better dabs and cod. The local stock of razorfish was killed by the severe winter of 1963, and a good bait for soles was therefore lost. Soft crab is a good all round bait, and can be gathered in season from the creeks around Gibralter Point, and sandeels are occasionally to be found. Shellfish baits, shrimp, and, strangely enough, silver rag and king rag, are not highly regarded locally.

BAIT SUPPLY. Lugworm is available, ordered three days in advance, from (winter only) 348 Roman Bank, Skegness. Herrings are usually kept by local fishmongers, and fresh mackerel can sometimes be obtained from local boatmen, or feathered from pier or boat.

In summer lugworm may be obtained by writing to the above address, which will result in names and addresses of bait diggers who *may* be able help being forwarded (s.a.e. please).

TACKLE DEALERS.—' Palmer ', 11 High Street, Skegness, Prop. L. H. and M. Dent. C. A. Marvin, Pet supplies and fishing tackle, 12 and 14 Lincoln Road, Skegness. Agents for local bait suppliers.

LOCAL CLUBS. Skegness Pier Angling Club. Hon Secretary, C. Hill Esq., 10 Lancaster Avenue, Skegness. The Club, which is a flourishing one, organises an eight-day Festival annually, usually in October. Details from Secretary concerning this and other "open" matches.

The Club also produces at irregular intervals an excellent guide to the sea fishing prospects in the area. This is available from the Secretary. Either he or Mr. A. E. Hewison of 5 Winthorpe Avenue will witness and weigh good fish.

The Skegness Sea Angling Club. Secretary: S. Kinning Esq., ' Westward Ho ', Everingtons Lane, Winthorpe, Skegness. The club organises, amongst its regular programme of ' open ' matches from beach and points, a two-day Beach Festival, and an ' Open ' Beach Anglers Championship. Details from Secretary.

LOCAL ADVICE. Mr. A. E. Hewison, Grocers Shop, Winthorpe Avenue, Skegness, and Colin Hill, 10 Lancaster Avenue, Skegness, will be pleased to offer advice and assistance to visiting anglers.

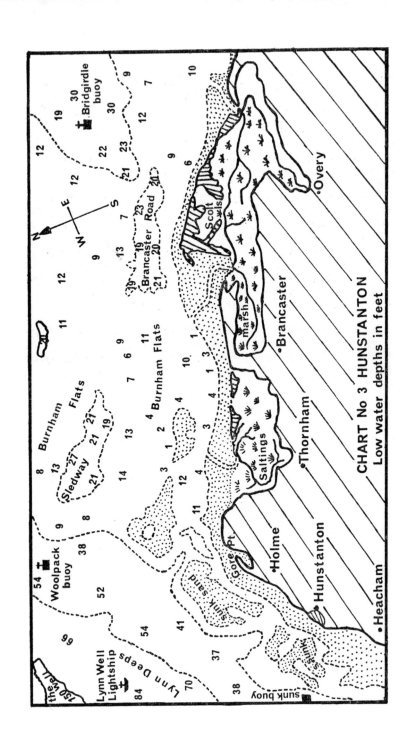

CHART No 3 HUNSTANTON
Low water depths in feet

2. The Wash and District

THE WASH. (CHART NO. 3)

Once the southern limit of the beach fishing already described in the Skegness area is reached, the coastline of the Wash itself is very unfriendly as far as the angler is concerned. Almost the whole length of it, round to Heacham, is either accessible only via complicated and dangerous routes through the saltings and marshes, or the tide travels so far out over extensive sands that fishing is not worthwhile. The tide comes in so fast that fishing would be a moving business, and under some circumstances extremely dangerous from the point of view of being cut off. For the brief period either side of high water when little walking out to the tide line would be necessary, the only prospect is a flounder or two and eels. Wildfowlers are active in the saltings and marshy areas of the Wash, and evidence of the tricky nature of the coast is apparent from the number of inexperienced wildfowlers who have to be rescued, by helicopter and rescue teams, from the area. The beach fishing is really insignificant and not worth the risk.

Boat fishing, too, is rather limited. The visiting angler, were he in the first place lucky enough to find someone ready to take him out in a boat, would find that from the inland harbours or ports the journey to sea is such a long and complicated one that it would be hardly worth while. Party boat angling is not organised until the Hunstanton area is reached, and the commercial fishermen of, say, Boston, would require a great deal of money to take a party of anglers out instead of carrying on their normal business.

BEACH FISHING (General notes). Some beach fishing is carried on on the Northern areas of Stubborn Sand, at Heacham. Cod and whiting do not frequent this area, so that the fishing is not really typical of most of the area covered in this book. Flounders, dabs, eels and some smoothhound are taken by anglers who walk out at low tide and note the positions of gulleys, etc., which are likely to contain fish on the flooding tide, and who then fish the tide up. Flounders and dabs are present throughout the year and are the mainstay of the beach angler's sport here.

HUNSTANTON. (CHART NO. 3)

Tides: +4hrs 45min H.W. London Bridge.
With the presence of mackerel inshore at times, and the tope, smoothhound, stingray and thornbacks which are all weighty

summer species, Hunstanton offers a better holiday season angling prospect than almost any other East Coast area. Such is the nature of things that the winter cod and whiting are almost entirely absent, and Hunstanton does not enjoy the peak fishing which the cold months bring everywhere else, south of the Wash.

Hunstanton Beach commences in the south with a man-made earth ridge locally known as 'The Hump' and forming the boundary with Heacham. Fishing the sands here is possible at all states of the tide, and at high water from the concrete promenade which stretches for half a mile or so north to the sewer outfall at Hunstanton south beach slipway. From the slipway to the cliffs at the northern end of the town, the sands, the Town Pier and, at high water, the promenade, again offer quite good prospects.

Between high and low water marks, about half a mile on the biggest tides, the beach is of flat, hard-packed sand. It is very heavily populated in summer by holiday crowds. At low water mark rocks and mussel beds are sometimes exposed. The pier stands dry on the bigger tides of twenty feet or more, but fishing is possible at all times on the more moderate seventeen and eighteen footers.

The whole stretch of beach is safe, with the possible exception, on big tides, of the stretch in front of the cliffs to the north. Here one could be cut off, but there are plenty of ledges to which one could retreat with no more than inconvenience to suffer. Nevertheless it is always wise to check upon tides before walking too far along the beach to fish.

Access to the whole stretch of beach is normally quite easy, though naturally parking is a problem in summer.

With the accent on summer fishing, and the coincidence of this with the huge holiday population, the beaches are not heavily fished, The whole stretch is of steady quality, however, and fishing in the evenings or early morning on suitable tides could be productive anywhere. Some impressive fish have been taken in recent years by those locals who are interested enough to test the potential. They include tope (28lb), stingray (27lb), smoothhound (23¼lb), and thornback (10lb). Less weighty, but nevertheless good fish, include many flounders over 2lb, dabs well over 1lb, and eels to 2½lb. Only one cod has been reported on rod and line, a fish of under 2lb! Mackerel and scad offer good sport in summer, and the occasional small bass and huss complete the local prospect. The rocky area under the cliffs is locally considered to be a good all-round spot.

Tides can be strong, but on normal flood and ebb, grip leads up to 6oz will cope well enough. Spinning with light tackle is possible at high water from the pier or the promenade, and this is the most likely spot in the area covered by this book to have consistent sport from the shore with mackerel. July and August are the mackerel months.

BAIT. There are no restrictions on digging, though naturally it is expected that anglers will not leave dangerous and unsightly holes in the sands in view of the holiday makers who visit the town. A variety of bait is available at low water in many places along the beach. These include lugworm, ragworm, sandeels and shrimp, with peeler crab obtainable in season from the rock patches, and local cockles worth considering too.

TACKLE DEALERS AND BAIT SUPPLY. Coles Sports Centre, High Street, Hunstanton 2119. Hunstanton Sea-Sports, Le-Strange Terrace, Hunstanton.

CHOICE OF BAIT. The baits which are available naturally in the locality account for all species, and there are no local specialities as far as beach fishing is concerned. Fish strips, especially fresh mackerel when available, are good for the rays, tope and smoothhound, and peeler crab is acceptable to almost all species. Sandeels are available live, and can be tried whole for bass, though these usually run small, and will also account for thornbacks. Lugworm and king rag are good all-rounders. Though there are extensive mussel beds near the low water mark, and may be gathered from the pier piles, they are not highly regarded locally as bait.

BOAT FISHING. There are no local boats available for hire, either for party anglers or for the small boat man. There are ample facilities for the launching of small boats however, and provided the visitor takes into account the sandbanks offshore, the big tides and the weather, all of which point to the fact that expert local advice must be sought, there is plenty of good fishing to be had.

WASH TOPE FISHING. As this book is written, tope anglers in the Wash area are again enjoying excellent sport with the species which has really highlighted this area throughout the country. As well as the local record fish of 61½lb, taken by Mr. Guy-Morton in 1966, there have been many other tope which are heavy by any standards, and which draw anglers from all parts of the country. Two tope clubs operate in the area, these being The Wash Tope Club which is based in Hunstanton, and The Sportsman's Tope Club which operates from Brancaster, just outside The Wash itself. The details which space allows me to give will indicate to the reader that the tope are treated in a truly sportsmanlike way, and that many live to fight another day—in direct contrast to the treatment which is often meted out to tope in other parts of the country, I am afraid.

The following list of tope and date of capture indicate the overall consistency and high quality of the tope fishing. This year

(1968) has been particularly good, but full details are not available as the season is not finished at the time of going to press.

50lb 27 May 1960, W. Collison; 51½lb 22 May 1961, E. Lee; 49lb 9 June 1962, I. Fovarque; 42lb 1 Sept. 1963, A. Dilkes; 45½lb 30 May 1964, B. Proctor; 38lb (3 fish) 3 June 1965, ————; 61¼lb 3 June 1966, G. Morton; 51½lb 29 May 1967, D. Greef; 43¼lb 20 July 1968, D. Greef.

This information is by courtesy of The Wash Tope Club, and does, I believe, indicate the biggest fish taken annually by members of the club, or anglers taking part in ' Open ' matches.

As well as tope, smoothhound, stingray and thornbacks take the same baits on the same tackle. The following list indicates the size of specimens taken locally.

Smoothhound 23¼lb July 1960, R. Reynolds; Stingray 34lb August 1963, T. Moden; Smoothhound 23lb August 1967, M. Bray; Stingray 27lb August 1964, F. Fovarque; Thornback Ray, 21lb June 1968, P. Evans (local record).

THE WASH TOPE CLUB.   The club was formed in July 1960 by eight founder members, and there are now seventy on the roll. Full membership may not be claimed until a tope of either 30lb (boats) or 28lb (beach) has been caught by the applicant. Associate membership is open to anyone proposed by a full member.

Members of the club restrict themselves to a maximum line strength of 32lb, and every effort is made to return all fish alive to the water. After being played out, fish are always ' tailed '— never gaffed, and are kept in the water until weighing time, when a wet sack is placed over the gill covers whilst the fish is out of water. After weighing, fish are taken into deep water and held until lively enough to swim away. 95% success is achieved.

Fishing with the club, which holds, on overage, two ' Open ' events each month, costs about 15s per head per match. The club owns two fifteen-foot boats with outboard motors and trailers, and, in addition, several members make their privately owned boats available to visitors taking part in club ' Open ' matches. Departure is from the Pier north slipway. In addition to the pleasures of catching tope in good company, there are eleven club and ' Open ' trophies fished for annually. as well as various medals and tankards which are awarded. Details of the match programme for the coming year, and any other information, can be obtained from the club secretary:—

Mr. R. Reynolds, 14 Queen's Drive, Hunstanton. Tel: 2366.

Since there are no local boats for hire apart from those provided in matches, visitors who trail their own small dinghies are unlikely to be able to reach the outermost marks, especially as extensive sand bars and banks are exposed about one and a half miles offshore, and local knowledge is needed to negotiate them.

In addition to this, the stronger tides make fishing impossible except for about an hour either side of high or low slack water. This means that the visitor who wants to fish well offshore in marks such as Lynn Deeps and Lighthouse Hole, will be well advised to go with the club who know the area. Other productive marks are The Graveyard, The Sewer Gulley, Catlin Hole and the deeper water of Lynn Deeps near the lightship. In general, the club fishes marks within five miles offshore, but this is a large enough area for trouble in plenty to befall the unwary visitor.

LOCAL ADVICE. Mr. E. Lee, current Chairman of The Wash Tope Club, and proprietor of a butcher's shop in High Street, Hunstanton, will be pleased to weigh any fish caught locally, and to offer advice concerning local prospects and conditions.

SMALL BOAT ANGLING. Provided the small boat angler keeps a weather eye open and restricts himself to the area inside the sand banks which extend from Holme southwards, he can enjoy good boat fishing, especially in the warmer months, under safe conditions. This exposed tip of the Norfolk coast is open to winds from the south, west and north, however, and anything above force four in these directions is distinctly unsafe. There is no heavy boat traffic to contend with close in, and the offshore sands are visible from half tide downwards, so under normal circumstances there is no real danger in good weather.

Access to the beach is possible in four places, South Beach slipway (near caravan site), Boating Lake slipway, Sandringham slipway (just south of the pier), and the pier slipway on the north side. The area to the north under the cliffs can present danger in the shape of rocks and smaller sand bars, but the lighthouse is a prominent marker for this area, which can therefore be easily avoided. Use of all four slipways is free.

Tides are, as has been stated, strong, especially on springs. Up to a pound of lead will be needed to hold bottom during the biggest tides, but on neaps four to six ounces will be enough. Normal boat tackle, with running leger, will be found suitable. Fishing is normally carried on at anchor, but when the mackerel are in, drifting is profitable. Wire traces are necessary for tope, of course.

Naturally, the inshore marks offer rather less scope than the deep water outside the sandbars, but all the local species, including tope, can be taken by the visitor fairly close in. With a lack of winter cod, and whiting only small, the accent is always on the warmer months. Dabs and flounders are present throughout, and April to September gives the best of the fishing with the other local species.

TOPE TACKLE. Owing to strong tides, tope fishing is not carried on from drifting boats as it often is elsewhere. Ground tackle is used, with plenty of swivels and a wire trace incorporated, and fresh mackerel is frequently available, these being feathered as required. A favourite local bait is a small whole whiting, which can normally be caught on lug or fish strip, and a good alternative is a six-inch dab, freshly caught and 'rolled' nose to tail before being presented.

Since the average size of local tope is around the 30lb mark, adequate but not unsporting tackle must be used (see notes on The Wash Tope Club). The earliest recorded fish was taken on 15 April, and the latest of the season was on 12 October.

HUNSTANTON PIER. The pier offers fishing for all local species, but stands dry at low water on spring tides. On smaller tides, the period from half-flood to two hours after high water gives good mixed fishing for local species, and spinning for mackerel is possible at high water. A gulley which offers slightly deeper water runs diagonally out from the north corner. Normal ground tackle will be found suitable, and baits are as for beach and boat fishing. The pier is open to fishermen during daylight hours, and it is possible, I understand, to obtain access after dark, but this is not officially available. Visitors are advised to make enquiries at the pier during 'open' hours if they wish to fish late.

LOCAL CLUBS. The Wash Tope Club. Secretary, R. Reynolds, 14 Queens Drive, Hunstanton. Tel: 2366. Hunstanton Sea Angling Club. The club is, according to my information, currently lapsed.

HOLME-next-SEA. (CHART NO. 3)

About three miles north of Hunstanton, Holme-next-Sea is a village some distance inland from the sea. The beach which is named by the village is therefore not quite as easily accessible as at many other spots, and is not heavily fished. Access is via Beach Road which turns off from the main Hunstanton/Cromer road (A149) and to within 250 yards of the beach. From there it is necessary to leave the car and walk across sand dunes. The beach is of hard gently shelving sand, with small soft rock scarves, exposed at low springs.

Prospects from this beach are mainly with dabs and flounders, though some bass are taken in summer. There is always the prospect of other local species being caught, especially if tope and thornbacks were fished for thoroughly. Sea trout are netted in considerable numbers here, and turbot and brill are also taken occasionally. Since the beach is heavily populated in summer by visitors, daytime fishing can be rather difficult and not very en-

joyable. The roads, which in many other villages on the coast
are made up and finish virtually on the beach itself, are not in
evidence here. The beach is still in its natural state, and the
northern section is a Nature Reserve.

Average tides expose about a quarter mile of hard sand at
low water, and various baits are available from half tide downwards. Tides can be strong, especially on big springs, when more
than the normal 6oz of grip lead might be necessary.

BOAT FISHING. Provided there are no onshore or alongshore
winds to make things difficult, launching a trailed boat would
be easy from this beach, and it is accomplished. The access ends
well short of the beach, however, and a land trailer with a four-
wheel drive vehicle would be needed to get across the dunes.
With this problem to contend with, and with dangerous sand
bars about a mile offshore which present a real hazard in unfavourable winds, it is not a place to recommend to the visiting
boat angler. Certainly the angler who could overcome the launching problem would still need to seek expert local advice and
guidance concerning weather and tide conditions. Part of the
beach is, as already stated, a Nature Reserve, and the dunes in
this area are privately owned. Access must not be assumed a
right.

The area is visited by boats from Hunstanton and Thornham,
and some very good tope have been taken off Holme. Fish to
42¼lb, and many in the 30 to 35lb range, have been recorded.
Good thornbacks, smoothhound and stingray are also caught here.

BAITS. Lug, peeler, rag, cockles, mussels and some silver ragworm can be obtained at half tide and below.

BOATS. None are available for hire.

THORNHAM. Here there is a small creek which constitutes an
unprotected harbour, and which dries out on medium or spring
low tides. No boats are for hire, but the visiting angler could, if
he chose his tides very carefully, get out and back after fishing
offshore. Certainly there are good tope, thornback, etc., to be
taken, but again the area is a complicated one, not to be recommended to the visiting angler, and a potential deathtrap to the
novice boatman.

There is beach fishing at Thornham, mainly for flats and eels,
and the harbour inlet offers excellent flounders.

BRANCASTER. This rather more substantial harbour is also
dry at low springs, but local boatmen do operate here, and it is
possible that the persistent visitor might arrange a trip out to sea.
The few boats which do operate are heavily booked in advance,

however, and no guarantee can be given. The Sportsman's Tope Club begins its trips here, and many extremely good tope and thornbacks are taken offshore. Owing to the very tortuous route out to sea, and the maze of sandbanks which lie offshore, as well as the big rise and fall of tide, it is not recommended that the visitor bring his own boat unless personal contact is made before-hand with someone who knows the area well.

BEACH FISHING.   There is some beach fishing to be had off Brancaster, mainly for flats and eels. The whole area is infested with crabs in the warmer months, and the fishing is over shallow sand. Large sea trout are netted commercially, but very seldom fall to rod and line. The occasional bass might be taken by anglers prepared to make the long walk to Scolt Head, which is a bird sanctuary, but from the angling point of view the trip, with fishing tackle, would probably be too arduous to be worthwhile.

SPORTSMAN'S TOPE CLUB.   The club owns no boats collec-tively, but several members put their's at the disposal of the club on fishing days. Most of these are large craft in the twenty-seven to forty-foot category, and they fish up to ten miles offshore. Local boatmen Derek Billing, Alf Large and others all co-operate closely in the activities of the club, and they have boats at Bran-caster.

Generally speaking the comments made concerning the Wash Tope Club (Hunstanton) with regard to tackle, baits and seasons apply here, except that the Sportsmans Tope Club has the advan-tage of being able to work further offshore when necessary, and in more adverse conditions. Some of the club's popular marks are the Lynn Well Lightship area, The Woolpack Buoy, Bridgirdle Buoy, and Brancaster Roads. In addition to ground tackle, float gear is often used, and again both small whiting and dabs are popular as bait in the early season before the arrival of the main mackerel shoals.

Highlight of the club's year is the International Tope Festival, which is well organised, successful, and which attracts entries from a very large area.

Miss Barbara Hall, of 'The Cabin' tackle shop in Kings Lynn, will give first-hand details to anyone calling at the shop, and the club secretary is: Mr. W. Weaving, 11 Hill Street, Hunstanton.

BOAT HIRE.   As stated, the boat hire situation is not currently easy as far as the stranger to the area is concerned, but it is possible that parties who wish to come, and can give advance notice, may be able to hire a boat and a skipper.

Mr. Derek Billing, 'Driftwood', Brancaster, is one boatman and Mr. A. Large of Brancaster another who might be contacted. Miss Hall at 'The Cabin', Kings Lynn may also be able to put anglers in touch with boatmen either at Brancaster or, for tope fishing of a similar nature in The Wash, from Kings Lynn harbour. In Hunstanton, Mr. G. Lee of Avenue Road, also caters for boating anglers.

BEACH FISHING. (Brancaster-Burnham-Overy-Holkham-Wells-Stiffkey-Blakeney.) The shoreline opposite these villages is not conducive to good beach fishing, though some spots such as Holkham do offer a limited amount of fishing for flats and eels. There are wide marshes to be negotiated between Wells and Blakeney, and the ebb tide goes out over extensive sands and cockle strands, which virtually rules out serious beach fishing.

BOAT FISHING. *Wells-next-the-Sea.* Tides: +5hrs 16min H.W. London Bridge. This somewhat larger and extremely attractive fishing village has a more substantial harbour and a thriving trade in shellfish is based here. Unfortunately there are no organised party angling facilities, but the whelk, shrimp and sprat fishermen will sometimes take out parties when there is no fishing or shellfish gathering on hand. Advance bookings are difficult to make, however, because of the commercial commitments of these men, and the visitor must, by and large, turn up and make immediate enquiries on the day.

The harbour is a very considerable distance from the sea itself, and in adverse winds it is doubtful whether the stranger who has put to sea in his own boat would be able to negotiate the narrow entrance through the sand bars at the extremities of the channel. This is, once again, a spot not to be recommended to the novice, and the experienced small boat angler must seek expert local advice. H.M. Coastguard Tel: Wells 219. (Not continuously manned.)

BLAKENEY. The route to the open sea from this small village is, if anything, more complicated still, and involves a journey of two to three miles from Blakeney itself, rather less from the small harbour at Morston. Again it is no place for the small boat angler.

Larger boats may be hired here, and the offshore fishing for summer species, tope, thornbacks, dogfish, etc., is good. Boatmen who operate full time for angling parties are listed for the general area under the Boat Fishing notes for Cley, which follow immediately.

TACKLE. Tides in the whole of this part of the Norfolk coast can be very strong, and up to 1lb of lead may be needed to hold bottom. Otherwise normal boat gear, with steel traces for tope, will suffice.

BAIT. The boatmen named can supply bait ordered in advance if it is required. This part of the Norfolk coast is rich in lugworm beds, and it is here that a great deal of the lug sent to many other parts of the country is obtained. The closure of minor railway stations has seriously affected delivery and cost in recent years, and the ever increasing demand from anglers keeps local diggers very busy. There is, in fact, speculation that the lugworm may eventually be dug out altogether.

3. Cley to East Runton

CLEY BEACH FISHING. The predominantly shingle beach at Cley offers quite good beach fishing, and is fairly popular with anglers in the winter, when cod and whiting are the attraction. In the past the beach has been a popular one for the holding of ' Open ' matches, two of which are the Norwich Sea Anglers event, and the Norwich Animal Health Trust match, both of which are held in September/October. The beach shelves fairly steeply, and is not too popular with holiday crowds in summer due to the lack of sand. During the summer months, mackerel shoal close in under favourable conditions, and heavy bags are taken by anglers who follow them with feather tackle or light spinners. The occasional tope, thornback, dogfish, etc., are taken from the beach, and fair bags of dabs at various times throughout the year. There are no real snags, though a wreck can be located at low tide and should be noted. That area has a reasonable reputation for dabs, though the somewhat featureless beach is of steady potential throughout its length. The wreck lies to the right of the access to the Beach. Normal tackle for the area will be found suitable at Cley, with tidal flow demanding grip leads up to 8oz for those who wish to anchor their tackle.

Access to the beach is straightforward, via Beach Road, to within fifty yards of the sea. There is ample free parking space.

BAIT. None is available from Cley beach, but nearby Blakeney is a source for the angler prepared to collect his own. Various bait diggers live at Cley and the surrounding area, however, and they will take advance orders. Details are given after notes on boat fishing.

BOAT FISHING. Morston, Blakeney, Cley Area. The offshore boat fishing in this area is full of potential, though there is not as yet a highly developed system of party angling on the Norfolk coast. Boats are available, however, and advance bookings can be dealt with. Local departure points are Morston and Blakeney, no large boats being available at Cley.

Anglers wishing to make arrangements for a day's fishing will find it essential to contact the boatmen beforehand, since times of departure and return depend very much upon the state of the tide.

At Morston, three boatmen with large boats capable of taking eight, possibly ten, anglers are: Mr. G. Bishop, The Bell, Wiveton.

Tel: Cley 523. Mr. R. Bishop, High Street, Blakeney. Tel: Cley 200. Mr. P. Green, 14 Church Street, Stiffkey. Tel: Binham 233.

At Blakeney, Mr. Long can be contacted and there are several big boats available. The address is Stratton Long, 'The Shingles', Westgate Street, Blakeney. Tel: Cley 362.

In each case the approximate cost per head, excluding bait, is 30s per day. A much larger fee will be expected from the angler who is alone, unless he is lucky enough to team up with other visitors for a day's outing.

Generally speaking, these large boats are available only between June and September. Catches include good tope, plenty of thornbacks, big dogfish, flats, plenty of mackerel on feathers, and occasional bass. There is a lack of local 'record' lists, but Mr. S. J. Jarvis has taken tope to 45lb, and Mr. E. R. Waller and Mr. G. Bishop are two other local boat anglers who have taken many good bags of fish. These gentlemen can be contacted for advice, and addresses are as follows: E. R. Waller, High Street, Cley, Norfolk; S. J. Jarvis, 4 Peacock Lane, Holt, Norfolk.

Neither Blakeney nor Morston are suitable departure points for trailed dinghies, owing to the long and very narrow channels which have to be carefully negotiated with expert knowledge. At Cley, however, the open beach is suitable along its length for the launching of small boats, provided, of course, that local weather conditions are taken very much into account. Deep water and good mixed fishing is available quite close in.

A limited number of outboard dinghies are available for hire at Cley. These ought to be booked in advance from: Mr. Williamson, Council Houses, Cley, Norfolk.

Good dinghies are available, each at £1 per day including motor, and fishing takes place during daylight hours.

For anglers wishing to bring their own boat, launching from the beach is free. Most dinghies depart from the area opposite the coastguard watch-house, near Beach Road. H.M. Coastguard Tel: Cley 313 (not continuously manned).

BAIT. As previously stated, bait can be ordered in advance from local bait gatherers, or obtained by the angler himself from the Blakeney area, at low tide. Local bait suppliers are: Ben Bishop, 'The Anchorage,' Cley; D. Howlett, Coast Road, Cley; H. Cornwall, Holt Road, Cley; B. Piggot, Council Houses, Old Woman's Lane, Cley.

The baits favoured locally are, of course, lugworm for the round fish, and mackerel strips for tope, dogs and thornbacks. Mussels and sandeels are also used with success. The angler digging at low water in the Blakeney area can obtain lug, sandeels, mussels, cockles and clam.

LOCAL CLUBS. Mr. E. Waller, 7 Queens Road, Holt, Norfolk, is Hon. Secretary of the Holt S.A.C.,

SALTHOUSE. Good beach fishing is continued at Salthouse, where the beach is still predominantly shingle, shelving quite steeply. The beach is very popular locally, and good bags of flats and cod, whiting, too, are taken in season. The odd tope, bass, thornback, etc., is also caught. Species and baits are as for Cley area.

Access is from the A149 to within a few yards of the water, and the beach is snag free, apart from the occasional rock patch. Local bait digger Bob Cook lives opposite the signposted left turn from the B149 two miles east of Cley. The deep water steep to the beach again allows anglers to take good bags of mackerel during favourable summer conditions, and the beach provides mixed fishing of a good standard. No bait is available locally, except through bait suppliers who dig, as described earlier, at Blakeney.

Access for dinghies is possible over the shingle bank, but there is no special slipway provided. Dinghy fishermen take good bags of fish, but as always caution is necessary and a constant eye must be kept on the weather.

Salthouse beach is reasonably popular with holiday makers, in spite of the fact that here and at Weybourne, the occasional land mine is still found. On the whole the beach is devoid of special features, and with a lack of shipping buoys or channels offshore, together with the fact that boat fishing is not developed to any great extent, there are no well-known marks.

KELLING. This beach offers prospects very similar to those at Salthouse. Access is from the A149, turning left at the police house which is on the right hand side of the road. In winter access is easy, apart from the fact that the ground gets very boggy, especially where small streams cross the lane to the beach. There is thus a possibility of becoming bogged down with the car, and it is wise to investigate the situation before going too far.

Baits, tackle, etc., are as for Salthouse, and the beach is of shelving shingle with sand patches.

WEYBOURNE. Two miles further along the A149, Weybourne again offers beach fishing into deep water, from a steeply shelving shingle beach. Access is via a left turn from the B149 near the 'Ship' public house, and is to within a few yards of the water. Ample parking facilities are available, and there is an opportunity to launch small boats over the shingle ridge. The beach is mainly clean and featureless, and the fishing from all points can be excellent. As is usual in this area, the highlight is the night fishing for cod and whiting in season, but calm summer conditions bring the mackerel in, and there is a good chance of a big tope at this time. The area under the cliffs, east of the access, is not as snag-free as the rest of the beach, and some tackle is lost in this

C

vicinity, by anyone who persists in using wire grip leads.

The beach is quite popular in summer, and is used for a camp at times by the army, but without restriction to anglers.

Offshore dinghy fishing offers a variety of mixed fishing, with considerable potential for big tope which is largely undeveloped at the moment. There is very deep water, and no threat from shipping. The steep beach can be very tricky to negotiate during swells or strong winds, however, and caution must be exercised by the visiting angler. No bait is available from the beach, but B. Cook, at Salthouse, can be contacted in advance, as can the men in the Cley area.

SHERINGHAM

Tides: +5hr 2min H.W. London Bridge.

The seaside holiday town of Sheringham offers beach fishing and a certain amount of boat fishing to the visiting angler, though the latter is by no means an organised facility.

BEACH. In summer, the holiday crowds in and around the town itself severely restrict the beach angler in daytime, though in any case the angling prospects are not great at this time in the year. Late evening anglers will take dabs, plaice, soles, eels, flounders, the occasional tope, brill and turbot, though never with notable consistency. In winter, however, the cod fishing can be very good, with individual fish to 18lb recorded, and plenty of fish of about 5lb average.

The beach is of shingle, with very uniform cobbles about four inches in diameter at high water mark, interpersed at low water mark and beyond with large patches of bigger stones. Most anglers prefer to fish the flood up, avoiding the snaggy nature of the low water ground.

The most popular part of the beach with local anglers is that to the west of the town, where fishing is carried on in front of the promenade, near the lifeboat shed, and round the 'corner' in a stretch known as 'Old High'. There are ample car-parking facilities, and charges are made in summer, with the exception of that in front of the Grand Court Hotel. The angler who inspects the beach at low tide will find that at the end of the breakwaters opposite the promenade there are deep and interesting gullies which run out at an angle from the beach and which, if carefully pinpointed, will obviously be productive, provided they can be reached with a lead.

The steep-to beach at 'Old High', as well as being a popular general spot, is ideal for approaching the mackerel with light tackle when they come inshore during the summer months.

To the east of the town, the shingle/sand/rockstrewn beach can again be productive to the beach angler. On both beaches grip leads are best avoided unless roughish seas or spring tides make them essential. Less gear will be lost if the angler uses a fairly heavy lead, leaves it strictly alone until the time comes to strike or retrieve, then, pointing the rod at the lead and taking up slack, does so as quickly as possible.

BAIT. A certain amount of lugworm is available at low water, but it is sparse at times, and cannot be relied upon. Shrimp can be gathered from the low water gullies in a push net.

Local bait suppliers are: Mr. B. Cook, Coast Road, Salthouse. Mr. B. Batrick, George Street, Sheringham.

Successful baits are as in other local areas, and fresh fish baits are best for the not uncommon brill and turbot which are a feature of Sheringham in spring and summer.

TACKLE. There are no tackle dealers as such in Sheringham, though one or two shops offer a selection. Tackle shops at Cromer are a source of supply, and larger towns further afield offer a wide selection.

BOAT FISHING. In spite of the fact that Sheringham is a holiday town, there is no well developed boat angling centre here. Local professional fishermen can be approached of course, and will take out parties on occasions. There are no dinghies especially provided for hire, though again personal enquiries may result in a boat being made available.

The visitor with a trailed dinghy will find access to the beaches straightforward enough, but the beach is not a friendly one in bad weather, and very great caution must be exercised. Low water presents problems as far as rocks are concerned, and the dinghy angler must be very careful in this respect. The offshore fishing is good, and notable mixed bags are taken of all the species common in the area, plus the brill and turbot which are unusual fish as far as anglers on the coasts of East Anglia are concerned.

Two local Fishery Protection Officers who will give advice concerning local conditions are: Mr. R. C. Rushmer, 'Craigbrook', Brook Road, Sheringham. Tel: 2634. Mr. H. K. Pegg, 'Salcombe', Norfolk Road, Sheringham. Tel: 2769. Hon. Secretary, Sheringham S.A.C. is Mr. Jonas, South Street, Sheringham.

BEESTON GAP. About one and a half miles east of Sheringham, the beach at Beeston Gap varies from sand to concentrated rock. As a source of soft crab and winkles, the keen angler will regard it highly with bait in mind, but a walk of at least half a mile is necessary from the nearest access point by car. The beach offers mixed fishing, but is, because of the limited access, not heavily fished.

WEST RUNTON. Half a mile further east along the A149, the beach at West Runton is, in general, a nightmare of rocky ground.

The determined angler who uses break-out tackle and expendable leads might do extremely well there with cod in winter, though most locals regard the beach as not worth fishing, especially to the west of the access, where the rocks are at their worst. The occasional bass is taken, however, and there are crabs to be found in the rocks. This is a place which seems to have potential for bass, and certainly for cod. A good look round at low water, and a careful approach to the fishing with suitable tackle might well produce surprises. The beach is heavily populated in summer by holiday makers. Professional fishermen can and will take out party anglers, and the offshore fishing is very good for the usual species.

EAST RUNTON.   Though still of a somewhat rocky nature, East Runton, some two miles short of Cromer, is an easier prospect for the beach angler. Access is again from the A149 and though parking is restricted in summer, it is adequate and free in winter, when the whiting and cod fishing is at its best. Catches are well up to the average for the area, and it is a popular winter night beach. Sparse lugworm beds exist, and shrimp and soft crab can be found here. It is advisable to do without wire grip leads, and to use break-out tackle after looking around at low water to note the position of rocks, which can alter during gales and heavy seas. The area to the left of the sewer pipe is particularly rocky. Once again, dinghy fishing is possible with the weather very much in mind, and very careful attention must be paid to submerged and isolated rocks when launching and returning. Offshore prospects are very good, with all the usual species, plus the odd turbot and brill to be taken.

BAIT.   Apart from what can be gathered from the beach, bait can be ordered in advance from the diggers mentioned for the Sheringham and Cromer areas.

4. Cromer and District

CROMER. (CHART NO. 4)

Tides: +5hr 10min H.W. London Bridge.

Again a seaside holiday resort, Cromer is heavily populated during the summer months, and daytime fishing from the beaches is, if it were productive in any case, out of the question during good holiday weather. A possible exception is the third breakwater east of Cromer Pier, which offers deeper water and relative freedom from sunbathers.

The beach is a sandy and gradually shelving one, with large patches of rock at intervals all along its length. Access to the beach is easy, there being seven slopes and steps at intervals. Parking is allowed on the promenade during winter, but is charged for and restricted to the town during the tourist season.

Cromer is a beach which repays a careful inspection at low tide, for patches of rock can be noted. Fishing adjacent to them with break-out tackle will produce good bags of cod in season, especially at night. These outcrops of rock are also the haunts of the sea trout which are netted, but seldom hooked by rod and line anglers.

Most locals prefer the final three hours of the flooding tide, but good bags of fish have been taken at all stages. Amongst these are bass to 5½lb by Mr. A. Sergeant, and the same angler has taken excellent catches of cod from many spots in the area, no less than 500 fish to his own rod during the season of 1967/68.

Thornbacks are rare from this beach, as are brill, bass and turbot. Mackerel come in sometimes, especially horse mackerel (or scad) and these are taken by anglers fishing, as dusk falls in calm weather, with light tackle round the piles of the lifeboat shed (which is situated at the seaward end of Cromer Pier).

The summer fishing is not too productive, but the whiting and codling fishing during the winter leaves nothing to be desired.

BOATS. The many good tope taken in this area are a pointer to the boat fishing potential, largely unexplored, which exists off Cromer and other nearby beaches. Cromer boat angler Gordon Jessop has taken tope of 60lb and, recently, another excellent fish of 45lb. Tom Spurgeon and John Shipley are other very successful boat anglers who have accounted for excellent tope as well as notable catches of other species. Almost everything will be encountered offshore from Cromer, and, of course, the summer potential is excellent, since none of the crowded conditions on

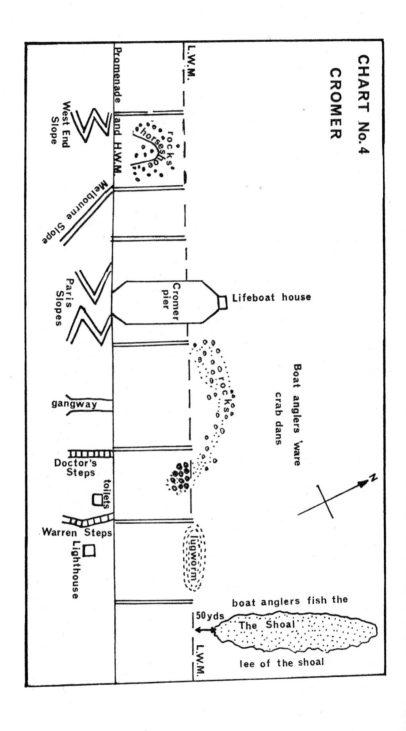

CHART No.4
CROMER

Promenade and H.W.M.

L.W.M.

West End Slope

Melbourne Slope

rocks 'horses'

Paris Slopes

Cromer pier

Lifeboat house

gangway

rocks

Boat anglers 'ware crab dans

Doctor's Steps

toilets

Warren Steps

Lighthouse

lugworm

N

boat anglers fish the

50yds

The Shoal

L.W.M.

lee of the shoal

the popular beaches have to be contended with. It would in fact be hard to find a better all round centre for boat fishing than Cromer. Unfortunately it is also a coast very much exposed to vicious weather which can hamper boat activities at any time of the year, particularly for the small boat angler.

Mr. 'Tim' Riches, Secretary of Cromer S.A.C. is a fund of local information, a very keen angler, and a useful man to contact if Cromer is chosen as a venue. Since there are not greatly developed party angling facilities, a stamped addressed envelope to Mr. Riches is a good idea so that the latest position can be obtained. Generally speaking, however, it is the visiting boat angler who trails his own small boat who is most likely to get to grips with the fishing off Cromer itself. It cannot be over emphasised that local advice *must* be sought concerning weather conditions, tides and general prospects. H.M. Coastguard Tel: Cromer 2507.

Launching facilities exist in two main places. These are the Gangway to the right of Cromer Pier, where anglers often reverse down the slope with the trailer attached, unhooking the boat at the bottom, and Melbourne Slope, well to the left of the pier. In summer permission to use this slope must be obtained by the beach inspector, but in winter that precaution is not necessary.

Garage owner Gordon Jessup, who has been mentioned earlier in connection with his knowledge and fine catches, lives near Melbourne Slope, and could be contacted for advice concerning conditions on the day.

There are not a great number of well-known local marks, since the boat fishing is not fully explored, but the chart given does indicate the presence of a sandbank, the lee of which (one side or the other, depending upon the tidal direction) has provided many good bags to boat fishermen, including tope to 35lb.

Small boat anglers are reminded of the hazard of rocks at launching and returning, and a look around at low water would be time very well spent. There is no shipping hazard or offshore snag, except the general presence of rock. Trip your anchor!

BOAT TACKLE.   Conventional running leger or paternoster gear is favoured, with leads up to 1lb being necessary once one fishes well offshore. As an average however, 6 ounces would be enough in conjunction with lines or around 18lb or so. Drift fishing is not practised, due to the rocky bottom, but there is little doubt that rubby dubby tactics and float or mid-water gear would account for tope, and drift fishing would be quite feasible.

BAIT.   Shrimp can be gathered from the rock pools, and some soft crab is available under the rocks. Low tide will reveal mussels under the pier, and some lugworm are available immediately opposite the light house. All these baits are successful from the beach, and mussel is a close second to the favourite lugworm, a fact which indicates that anglers in other areas ought to give it far more trial than they ever do.

Randall's (Gifts) Limited, Church Street, Cromer, and F. Pearce, Sports Outfitter, Church Street, Cromer, will take orders for bait in advance. Randall's supply, in addition to lugworm, mussels in season, and deep frozen clams, herring, sandeels, etc.

CRAB POTS—A warning to boat anglers.

Owing to the rocky nature of the sea bed, much commercial crab taking is practised. Cromer crabs are famed throughout the country in fact. The location of the pots is marked by buoys (dans) which rise to the surface at each end of a 100-yard run of pots, lying on the sea bed. Apart from causing disturbance and ill-feeling between anglers and commercial fishing, which is certainly not in the angler's interests, gear is likely to be lost if boat fishermen anchor near the dans. Crabbing is practised all along the beach between Cromer and Bacton, and a careful look out for the dans must be maintained. In addition, night lines are often set by beach liners in search of fish. The fishermen sometimes mark the positions of their lines with lights or obvious posts, beach anglers could have difficulty with them.

CROMER PIER.   The pier is open all the year round at all times of the day and night, and the current charge is 1s 2d per rod per session. The pier produces excellent catches of cod and whiting in season, and the east end has something of a reputation as a 'cod corner'. All the other species are taken at odd times, and specimen fish of one kind or another are often turning up. One of the photographs shows Mr. A. Hoolhouse with a fine plaice of nearly 4lb, taken from the pier in May.

As far as I personally am concerned, the most interesting and exciting prospect is the splendid tope potential of Cromer Pier. Excellent fish are taken every season, two of 29lb and 35lb falling to Mr. A. Sargeant within half an hour of one another in July 1965. 'Tim' Riches took a grand 40lb fish in 1963 to win a competition, and has had other smaller ones. Herring strip is the usual bait, with fresh mackerel and, if obtainable, small live dabs, pouting etc., are well worth trying. Most anglers use either a running leger or a single boomed paternoster with a long flowing trace or alternatively, a French boom. Grip leads are necessary at times.

Other good fish to come from the pier include bass of 10lb 1oz by Mr. N. Smith in October 1965, and cod well into double figures just now and again.

The use of naked lights on the pier at night is forbidden.

TACKLE DEALERS.   A good selection of tackle suitable for local use is available at Randall's, Church Street, The Hobby Shop,

West Street, and F. Pearce, Sports Outfitter, Church Street, Cromer.

LOCAL CLUBS. Tim Riches is Secretary/Treasurer of Cromer S.A.C. His address is 17 Lynewood Avenue, Cromer, Norfolk.
Other well-known anglers who are able to give sound local advice are:
Terry Pearce, 6 Marrams Avenue, Cromer, Norfolk.
Mr. F. Goffin, 64 Orchard Close, Norwich, Norfolk.
Mr. A. Hoolhouse, 49 Crossdale Street, North Repps, near Cromer, Norfolk.

OVERSTRAND. The first beach east of Cromer is that at Overstrand, and access is fairly easy some three miles along the A149, by turning left down one of the several lanes which lead to the car parks. Access to the beach itself is via a gangway. The beach is a sandy one, gradually shelving, and heavily populated during summer by holiday crowds, when parking can be a problem.
All the normal species for the area are taken here, with the accent once again on cod and whiting in autumn and winter. Good bags of dabs and flounder are taken at various times, and the very occasional brill turns up too.
Generally, the left side of the gangway is reckoned to be more productive to the beach angler, and the area between the break-waters near the steps is well fished. Lugworm can be dug at low tide but they are small, and not always plentiful. Again, the area to the left is the best lug ground.
Tides are moderate, and fishing without grip leads is often possible. Normal beach tackle for the area will be found suitable.

SIDESTRAND. Between Overstrand and the next beach, Trimmingham, Sidestrand beach has no public access. Fishing is quite possible and productive for those prepared to make the fairly long walk involved.

TRIMMINGHAM. This beach, some five miles south-east of Cromer and about seven from North Walsham, is not quite so easily approached by car, due to the restriction of a rather poor road. A new road is being constructed in the vicinity of the caravan site there, and although this will make access easier, the beach will probably be more heavily populated by visitors in summer as a result. Again the beach is of gradually shelving sand, with gullies exposed at low springs.
The beach is approached from the A148 just past the radar station which lies on the right side of the road travelling from Cromer. A gangway leads to the beach with a bomb disposal unit on the left, private caravan site on the right. At this point the North Norfolk Cliffs are at their highest, having begun at Weybourne. In previous years the beach to the left was a prohibited area, but has now been reopened to the public.

Tackle, species and general prospects are as for Overstrand, and lug is again available at low water in limited quantities. The beach is excellent for codling in winter, and some excellent soles are taken in season.

MUNDESLEY.   The A148 ends at the village of Mundesley, and appropriately enough, the beach provides some of the best general fishing to be had in the area. It is an outstanding cod beach, Alan Sargeant of Cromer having taken up to twently-seven fish at a session, and some very good bags of soles are made here. Thornbacks are by means unknown, the occasional good tope is landed, and most other local species are encountered at times. Local anglers John Barker and Graham Gotts have taken good catches of almost all species from this beach. The best regarded areas are in front of the Manor Hotel, and then towards Trimmingham. Fishing can be good at any state of the tide, not excepting low water, but the flood is more generally favoured. Normal beach tackle for the area, with grip leads occasionally necessary, though a certain amount of rock can give trouble in that respect.

In addition to guest houses and chalets in the vicinity, there are also caravan sites. The area is therefore heavily populated during the summer months.

Lugworm can again be dug at low spring tides, though the worms are sparse and continually on the move. Whilst digging bait, the angler should take the opportunity of looking round at low water to locate rocks and gullies which need pinpointing to increase catches.

Access is at two points from the B149, one in the vicinity of the coastguard lookout, and the other adjacent to the 'Ship' public house. The latter access is a landmark for fairly regular lug beds on the beach opposite at low water, the other main area being well to the left of the Manor Hotel. Here there is a stretch of beach which seems to be regularly visited by thornbacks in season, and night anglers take them on occasions. Dabs are to be taken at all points, as are cod and, to the right and left of the coastguard access, good soles.

Cars can obviously get no nearer to the beach than the cliff tops, and there is a car park provided in the area near the amusement arcade in the village.

BOAT FISHING.   Off-shore boat fishing is again unexplored, but is obviously full of potential. Local fishermen will take anglers out, but none operate on a large scale with anglers in mind.

TACKLE DEALERS.   None at Mundesley, but those at Cromer are available, plus Webb's (Tackle) Ltd., Market Place, North Walsham.

BAIT SUPPLY.   As for Cromer.

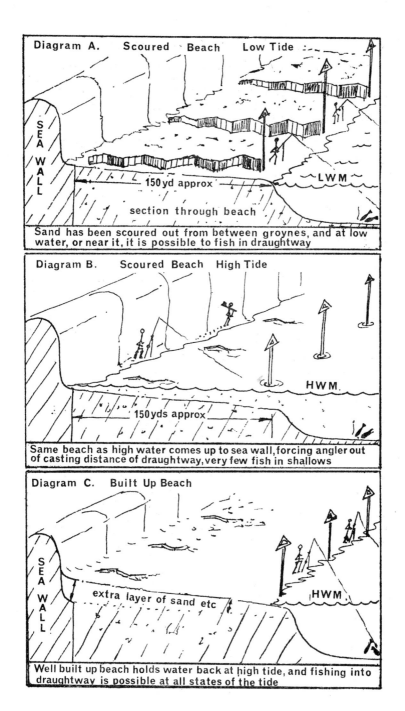

Diagram A. Scoured Beach Low Tide

SEA WALL

150 yd approx

section through beach

LWM

Sand has been scoured out from between groynes, and at low water, or near it, it is possible to fish in draughtway

Diagram B. Scoured Beach High Tide

150 yds approx

HWM

Same beach as high water comes up to sea wall, forcing angler out of casting distance of draughtway, very few fish in shallows

Diagram C. Built Up Beach

SEA WALL

extra layer of sand etc

HWM

Well built up beach holds water back at high tide, and fishing into draughtway is possible at all states of the tide

SANDBANKS. South of Mundesley, there are extensive offshore sandbanks which have a considerable effect upon sea anglers From now onwards, visiting anglers will be well advised to bear these in mind, and to remember carefully the information given in the following notes.

NORTH NORFOLK COAST AND OFF-SHORE SANDBANKS.

At this stage it is necessary to inform any intending visitor to this part of the coast that many beaches in the area need to be considered in the light of tidal and wind action, and their combined effect upon the beach and the extensive sandbanks which lie off shore for many miles along this coast.

Both boat and beach fishing is coloured by the existence of these banks, and at the outset it is worth pointing out that anyone off shore in a dinghy can easily find himself in desperate trouble if nasty seas begin to break over the banks between his boat and the shore. There are no natural harbours to run for, and if sea conditions outside the bank are also worsening, the situation can easily be very threatening. For this reason I deliberately play down the sport available in the hope that the angler who visits any of these beaches with a trailed boat will first seek local advice. Boat fishing is carried on, there are slipways, and access to the beaches themselves are often easy enough. I mention these where applicable, but as a general indication of how tricky the negotiation of the surf and banks can be, I quote Fred Williams, who knows the area like the back of his hand, who states that in an average year the competent dinghy angler might expect to find conditions suitable on only sixty-five days during that period.

Beach fishing too is always carried on with the state of the bank and the beach in mind. Most locals will agree that the ' draught way ,' which is the gully between the ends of the groynes let in the beach, and the sandbank anything from 100 yds to 400 yds offshore, is the most likely place for feed and fish to accumulate. Unfortunately it is not always possible for the angler to get his bait into the draughtway. Whether he will be able to or not depends upon the weather prior to his visit, and the state in which that weather has left the beach. All too often it is scoured of sand, and an extensive flat ' table ' covered with enough water to prevent wading, and not enough to attract fish, lies between the angler and the draughtway. (See diagram A on page 43.) When this situation prevails fishing the flood tide is a waste of time, and the angler must wait for the ebb to enable him to reach the draughtway from the seaward end of the exposed groynes. (See diagram B).

Thus it is that for much of the year, two hours or more after high water, through the ebb, and halfway up the flood is the only period worth fishing.

During more favourable spells, that is to say during long periods when there is no north or east in the wind, the beaches build up to cover the groynes completely, and it is therefore possible to fish into deeper water at all stages of the tide. (See diagram C).

BACTON. The next beach south of Mundesley is Bacton, a name rapidly becoming familiar throughout the country as the place where North Sea Gas is being piped ashore. Anglers will be pleased to learn that the pipes and refinery cause very little restriction to them, and some two miles of beach is available between here and Walcott.

The beach is easily accessible, there being roads at each end of the village of Bacton, as well as one in the centre. There is ample parking space, and parking is either free or payment optional.

Bacton fishes, on the whole, a little better than some beaches in the area, though this statement is made with the proviso that the angler concerned understands the importance of fishing at the right state of the tide, as was explained in the general notes a page or two previously. There is sometimes a good run of thornbacks in spring and again in late summer, and some of the fish taken are very big indeed. A Norwich angler took one of 23½lb here in 1961, and several good bags of smaller fish are taken by those who know the beach. Night fishing is generally more productive for all species than daytime fishing, but it is not essential for a degree of success. The beach is moderately popular with holidaymakers. The autumn and winter months provide good codling fishing. though real heavyweight specimens, in the 20lb class, are very rarely taken. Soles are also taken during the summer months, with a sprinkling of other species from time to time. Dabs and flounders are consistently taken, the former especially in April/May and the winter months.

The metal groynes are zig-zag in shape, and punctuate the length of the beach at 200-yard intervals, each groyne being around 150 yards long. The beach is predominantly sand, with a percentage of shingle and large flat stones. The southern end is generally considered to be the best end from the angler's point of view, probably because it is this end which tends to build up most rapidly after bad winds have scoured out the sand and made fishing mediocre. As stated earlier, it is when the beaches are built up that fishing is best, and it may seem odd to the visitor that heavy gales do not build up the beach. Instead a heavy undertow is caused, and sand is scoured out of the beach and dropped on the seaward sandbanks. This in turn allows the tide to come right up to the sea wall, and prevents the angler from getting out to the ends of the groynes to cast into the deeper draughtway. A further study of diagrams A, B and C on page 43 will clarify this point.

It is worth mentioning that observation at low tide will often reveal the lowest area of the offshore sandbank, and fishing opposite this spot puts the angler near to the area where fish and food come into the draughtway from the open sea. Fishing opposite the higher parts means that the angler is banking on taking fish which are running along the draughtway. This is often profitable of course, but local experts do look very carefully at the bank, especially on low springs. There is a slipway for dinghies opposite the road leading down to the beach, forming the middle one of the three access points. Dinghy anglers are reminded that this area is dangerous however, and local advice must be sought. Mr. M. Hodson, Eastways, Bacton, will give advice to visitors.

BAIT. Small quantities of lug can be dug at low tide, mainly on spring lows. Larger quantities are available at Mundesley. Brown shrimp can be taken with a push net at many beaches in this area, again at low tide, and these should never be overlooked as a choice of bait.

Bait, including frozen herrings, can be supplied by M. Hodson, Eastways, Bacton, who also supplies tackle.

Further afield, there are two more tackle dealers who may be contacted. John Roper, Station Road, Wroxham, supplies bait and fishing tackle. Tel: Wroxham 2453, after hours, 2838. Ken Latham, of Potter Heigham, has one of the largest selections of fishing tackle at his 'Angler's Paradise'.

WALCOTT. The B1159 coast road from Bacton gives easy access to Walcott beach in many places, and this accounts for its popularity amongst sea anglers. Still predominantly sand, the beach is again punctuated with tubular steel groynes at 200-yard intervals. The general remarks made earlier concerning the scouring effect of wind and tide apply very much here, and it is a sad fact that for much of the year the beach is flatter than most anglers would prefer it to be. Nevertheless it rewards the persistent angler with average results for the area, though beach fishing along this whole stretch of coast is a pastime in which results are hard won.

Night fishing is again more productive, though the winter codling fish well throughout the day on favourable tides. Thornbacks are a noted species from this beach, and Fred Williams has had some extremely good bags, as have other local experts. In the rare summers when the beach remains built up, and thornbacks are running, Fred has averaged fish on eight occasions out of ten. As any beach thornback angler will agree, this is good fishing. It cannot be emphasised too strongly however that the casual visitor is unlikely to meet with startling success.

When the beach is not built up, best results with thornbacks will be obtained as the tide is leaving the beach, especially when this coincides with darkness. Local angler Tom Goodly likes this combination, and has done extremely well in the past. Thornbacks are at best unpredictable however, and cannot be relied upon in any one season to turn up night after night.

The remarks applicable to Bacton also suit Walcott, and extend to bait supplies and tackle as well. In addition to cod and skate, the beach fishes well at times for dabs and flounders, with mackerel and other summer species putting in the occasional appearance.

BOAT FISHING. There is a slipway at the southern end of Walcott Wall which may be used for launching trailed boats, but once again the visitor is reminded that he must take local advice on this dangerous beach.

Peter Webster runs a fishing boat here, and Tom Goodly is an experienced rod and line boat angler too. Catches of good cod, thornbacks, some big tope, dogs and flatfish are taken from boats, and provided the weather is settled and advice is sought beforehand, there are excellent prospects for the visiting boat angler. The boat fishing is understandably limited by local conditions however, and only those people on the spot can give reliable advice.

Boatman: Mr. Peter Webster, 11 Paston Road, Bacton. Tackle dealers and Bait: as for Bacton.

ACCOMMODATION. The Coastline Holiday Village, Ostend, Walcott, is, of course a summer facility, catering mainly for holidaymakers. The angler wishing to enjoy winter cod fishing from local beaches will, however, be interested to learn that extremely reasonable winter rates apply in the hiring of the chalets, which are very comfortable, and only a few yards from the beach and good fishing. A brochure will be sent upon inquiry at the above address, or telephoning Walcott 491. This would be an ideal base for a group of hardy winter beach anglers.

OSTEND is the southern continuation of Walcott beach, and is considered as separate mainly because it differs slightly in character. It builds up again after bad weather more rapidly than the beaches to the north, and as such fishes more easily at all states of the tide. The disastrous floods on the East Coast in 1953 wreaked havoc all along these beaches, and the continuous war against eroding powers of tide and storm is still a feature of local life. A great concentration of groynes exists here as well, and they have done much to curb the erosion of the sea wall and the cliffs between here and Happisburgh. Fred Williams speaks with emphasis when he remembers that during his own years of fishing these beaches he has watched the sea eat inland for over a 100 yards towards Ostend House, a local landmark on the cliff top. He also recalls how a certain Mr. Grimmer used to cut steps down the forty-feet high cliffs in a new spot each year, to enable him to get down for the fishing. Access these days is from four points. A signposted back road at the Walcott end of the beach gives three points of access, and cars may be left at the beach ends of these three small roads. Anglers using the steps alongside Ostend House are reminded that this is a privilege allowed at the moment by the owner, and not to be abused.

The fourth access is at the southern end of Walcott Wall, and there are no more between Ostend and Happisburgh.

Ostend beach fishes on a par with others in the area, and a few big tope and dogs sometimes turn up in May and June. Visiting anglers would give a great deal to have the kind of sport enjoyed on one May day many years ago, by the late George Howlett of Great Yarmouth. An experienced angler, and a great believer in peeler crab, Mr. Howlett used this bait to take over 150lb of thornbacks, in daylight, and with his single rod and line. These were hauled up the cliff by rope! Another remarkable fish to come from this area was a conger eel reputed to weigh 150lb, and found by the Mr. Grimmet mentioned earlier, at nearby Walcott. Fred Williams has a photograph of him with this enormous eel, nearly 60lb over the present British record!

Ostend is also a good codling beach, and whiting too are taken in autumn. The usual lesser species are present, dabs fishing quite well and flounders too, both throughout the year. Bass, mackerel, soles and plaice are also caught at times.

Though the beach builds up more rapidly than other beaches in the area, it is still an excellent idea to look round at low tide, noting the high and low spots of the offshore sandbanks, as has been explained earlier in this chapter.

BAIT.   Small quantities of lug can be dug at low tide, and brown shrimp is available at the same time to the angler using a push net. Bait supplies as for Walcott and Bacton.

BOAT FISHING.   Not a great deal of boat fishing is carried on here, the only access for boats being on a slipway at the northern end of the beach. Anglers using it are reminded that local advice concerning prevailing conditions must be sought.

LOCAL INFORMATION.   Fred Williams of 30 Ordnance Road, Great Yarmouth, and his angling associate Walter Weldon will pass on information to the angler contemplating a visit to Ostend. Fred Williams is of the opinion that in spite of the lack of local specialisation, this beach has potential as a bass beach. Fred and two friends have taken up to twelve fish in a day, though not, it must be emphasised, every day! Fred's best fish to date is a 10¼ pounder, taken on kingrag.

There is no local sea angling club.

TACKLE DEALERS.   As for Walcott and Bacton, with others to be given as Great Yarmouth is covered.

HAPPISBURGH (Haisboro).   South of Walcott and Ostend, the B1159 curves away from the sea for a short distance, to run closely again at Happisburgh, and the lighthouse there is a familiar landmark. Still ravaged by the sea in spite of groynes, heavy wooden revetments and the sea wall, this beach is a tricky one to fish well, and on the whole is perhaps less productive than others in the area.

Access is easy, and there is ample free parking space. One access is a lane running past an inn called ' Hill House ' which is reached by turning left off the B1159 from Walcott. Further along the B1159 there is a signposted left turn marked for the beach. Turning down here, one either carries straight down to the southern access, or takes another left turn to reach the beach in the vicinity of the lifeboat station, where one of the fastest inshore lifeboats is housed.

The northern part of the beach is the best fishing area, since a good build up of sand and shingle means that fishing is possible on the flood tide well away from the bottom of the cliffs, into the deepest spot. Further south it is better to fish only the ebb tide, since the beach is often badly scoured out, allowing the flood to advance quickly and provide only shallow water. Night fishing is undoubtedly more profitable, and thornbacks are sometimes taken in season, together with good cod in winter, the occasional tope, and some very good bags of dabs. Flounders may be caught at any time of the year, a few bass, eels and dogfish also during summer and early autumn. Tackle of the normal kind for the area is used, with grip leads up to six ounces sometimes necessary. Baits too are normal for the area, and there are a few lug to be dug from the sandbanks which are occasionally exposed on low spring ebbs.

BOATS. Access via the northern ramp opposite the lifeboat station is available for dinghies, and the few boats which are used from this beach do well. There are no general marks which provide exceptional fishing, but about 400 yards from the shore opposite the lighthouse there is a wreck which is covered during the flood, and could be a considerable hazard to boats if its presence were not remembered. The usual precautions must be taken by visiting boat anglers concerning offshore surf caused by sandbanks, and the possibility of adverse weather. The southern access does have a boat ramp, but there is no corresponding gap in the revetment at that point, as there is at the northern one. H.M. Coastguard (Happisburgh) Tel: Walcott 273. Not always manned.

CART GAP. This, the next beach south, is well up to the average in terms of results, though it suffers in exactly the same way from the ravages of the sea. Access is clearly signposted, a left turn travelling south bringing one on to an unclassified road, which leads for 500 yards down to the beach. Access from there is via one of several gaps between the bungalows situated behind the marram hills and the sea wall, or over the ramp and slipway. A car park is available, and a small fee is charged, at least during

D

the summer. Neither this beach nor Happisburgh to the north are over populated, to date, at any time of the year, and both are fairly lightly fished.

This beach also produces good catches of thornbacks on occasions, and is good for codling from Christmas through to April. There are some broken groynes which can snag tackle, and these are naturally more often encountered after strong winds and seas have scoured the beach. At other times they are covered. Small quantities of lug can be dug from the sandbanks exposed at spring lows, and shrimp can be taken with a push net. Baits, tackle and leads are as for other local beaches, and apart from the notable cod and thornbacks, the other occasionally taken species are similar to those for adjacent beaches, with the possibility of good dab fishing worth noting especially. The three hours either side of high water is the best time, with the accent on night fishing.

BOATS. Access for dinghies is provided by a slipway at the end of the lane and near to the car park, but unfavourable winds are, as always, a constant hazard. Results are good, but the dangers are again emphasised.

ECCLES. The reader may learn with some relief that there is at least one beach which stands up reasonably well in this area to the constant scouring action of wind and waves, and Eccles does, for that reason, fish extremely well at times. Some tremendous catches of thornbacks have been taken here by Fred Williams and others, and it is worth noting some of them. Before I do so, however, I would remind the intending visitor that thornbacks are unpredictable fish, and conditions have to be to their liking before they will come in close enough for contact to be made by beach anglers. When they do fish well, however, they make no bones about it!

What must surely be a record for beach caught thornbacks on any English coast is that made ten years ago by Mr. Walter Weldon of Northgate Street, Great Yarmouth. Fishing late in July on the last half of the flood, Mr. Weldon took no less than twenty-four thornbacks which totalled over 200lb, and he still has the receipt for their sale on Lowestoft fish market! A few days previously, the same angler, together with Fred Williams and Mr. Flaxman of Flaxman's tackle shop in Great Yarmouth took twenty-five fish between them, and Fred has had personal bags of up to nineteen fish on a tide, best to date weighing 21½lb. Other bags of fifty-five fish between six anglers, and several of over a dozen per man are to be heard about still. Another point of interest is the faith which Mr. Basil Jeary of Lessingham has in push-net collected brown shrimp as a bait for thornback and cod. He has taken up to sixteen thornbacks on a tide, as well as some excellent bags of cod whilst using it. The visitor to the area would be well advised to chat with Mr. Jeary if the opportunity arises.

Few anglers fish specifically for big tope from these beaches, but several are taken by those who are using fish baits for thornbacks. Fred Williams has, during his thornback fishing, taken over twenty sizeable fish from beaches in this area, best 35lb, and there is little doubt that hard fishing for them would bring results. Big dogfish of around double figures are also encountered, and some excellent bags of dabs too. The beach fishes well in fact for all local species, and Mr. Florey of Sutton, has taken up to fourteen thornbacks as late as last week in October.

From the B1159, Eccles beach is reached by a left turn and further travelling of around one and a half miles, from the village of Lessingham. Three main access routes are available, the first by turning left down the Church Road, and the other two by forking either right or left at ' The Kennels ', where tea and coffee, etc., are served. The centre access has most car space available, either free or by voluntary payment of, at present, 6d. This is also the best access for those with boats. The beach is gradually becoming more popular, and is moderately populated in summer, but it is not, on the whole, too heavily fished. The Bush Estate is an area of privately owned bungalows and chalets, but the visitor could hire a caravan or chalet in the area, very close to the fishing.

Again a beach flanked by marram hills and sea wall to a height of around thirty feet the beach does, as stated, hold together fairly well. It can fish well in daylight, but night, coinciding with a rising tide, will almost certainly be more productive. The spring ebb leaves the beach very rapidly, and since the fishing area becomes very flat and shallow it is not usually worth fishing below half ebb. Moderate supplies of lug are available on the sandbanks exposed at low tides, and shrimp can be taken from the draughtway. The groynes are approximately 200 yards apart, and extend for about 150 yards out from the sea wall.

Tackle and baits are as for other local beaches.

BOATS. All the beach species, plus mackerel at times, can be taken from boats, and locals use skiffs for fishing in on occasions. The usual advice applies concerning trailed dinghies and the dangers of this coast, but more specific advice could be gained from Mr. Sam Kerrison, who lives at the White House near Castle Farm, which is along the right fork past ' The Kennels ' mentioned earlier. Mr. Kerrison has fished this beach for many years, and is well qualified to give advice to visiting anglers concerning prospects and dangers. As previously stated, there is a slipway near the car park. A general word of warning concerning the fact that small boats must be pulled well up into the marram hills and anchored will not go amiss. Very high tides could well carry away a boat left in an exposed position.

SEA PALLING. A distinctly sandier beach than others to the north, Sea Palling is also becoming more popular with visitors. It was badly affected when the sea broke through during the great flood of 1953, but is now building up again, and offers reasonable fishing. It is clear of groynes for about half a mile, and there is good access for trailed boats. Catches of thornback are made, as well as codling, especially after Christmas, and the other local species give sport as well. It is not a beach well known for heavy bags, but will probably yield better catches than hitherto if it becomes more popular.

Access is easy from the B1159, and the left turn between Lessingham and Waxham is signposted. A lane some 500 yards long, with two or three car parks along it, leads directly to the beach and slipway. 'The Lifeboat' public house, washed away during the floods along with several houses, has now been rebuilt and stands just behind the sea wall and marram hills.

BOATS. Boat fishing is possible, and profitable, but the normal warnings which have been emphasised so much concerning this area still apply.

WAXHAM. Though not heavily fished, Waxham beach is rapidly becoming more popular with both local and visiting anglers. As with one or two other beaches in the area, it offers the luxury of a few thornbacks in spring and autumn, and fishes well up to average for codling between October and April. Dabs and flounders often fish quite well, and good bags of spurdog are sometimes taken. Other species are less frequently caught though the familiar ones in this part of the world all turn up from time to time.

Access, whether approach is made from the north or the south, is via the lane which runs down to the beach from behind Waxham Church, with a telephone kiosk as an additional guide to turn left for those coming from the north. There is a car park quite close to the beach, but the short walk necessary to reach it is hard going, through a gap in high sand dunes opposite the car park.

War against the ravages of the sea is evident at Waxham as it is in other local beaches. The wooden groynes are supplemented by special plantations of marram grass which help to bind the sand and prevent it being swept away by wind and water. It is a punishable offence to damage the marram hills in any way, or to light fires on them.

The groyne area to the left of the approach gap remains built up more effectively than other parts of the beach, and the reader who has studied previous notes on the importance of this to the angler will have no difficulty in appreciating why this area is generally reckoned to fish best. Here the angler may fish at almost all states of the tide with the possibility of success. Locals consider that the last three hours of the flood, ideally combined with gathering darkness, are the most productive. Elsewhere along the beach, the offshore sand banks make it less profitable, due to lack of water in the draughtway, to fish between half-tide and the bottom of the ebb.

BOATS.   A little boat angling is done here, and some good tope are taken, as well as all the fish taken from the beach. Mackerel shoal within reach of dinghy anglers in summer, and heavy bags of fish have been made. Once again, however, though there is a slipway available, it is essential to consult locals before pushing off from the beach. Few longliners or longshoremen use this beach, though they sometimes net seatrout here. The sand banks are, as always, a menace to the boat angler, and must be treated with great caution.

BAIT.   Small quantities of lug can be dug at low tide both to the north and the south, and brown shrimp can be gathered in a push net from the draughtway at low tide.

TACKLE.   As for other local beaches.

HORSEY.   It is not within the precincts of this book to talk about coarse fishing, but Horsey is a name more than well known in the coarse fishing world. Horsey Mere recently produced the biggest pike caught in England, a forty-pounder, and it has seen the capture of many other very good fish, too. Within shouting distance almost, lies the sea, and considerable potential for thornback fishing in spring and autumn exists for the beach angler who studies conditions carefully. Fred Williams has taken up to eight fish on a tide, whose total weight bettered 72lb. Good beach fishing by any standards that, but the reader must not be misled into thinking that the beach regularly yields such catches. The condition of the beach alters rapidly, and again it is important to seeks out those spots where the beach remains built up, with the help of groynes and marram hills, rather than scoured clean of sand and left shallow.

There are two points of access, about half a mile apart, one at the north end of the village and the other more central. The northern access, turning left from the B1159 from Waxham, is rough surfaced, but negotiable by car. Coming through the gap at the end of it, the angler will find that the first space between groynes to the left is usually fairly well built up, and provides good fishing.

The next access, further south along the B1159, lies just past the telephone kiosk. Turning left here, and passing the ' Lord

Nelson' on the left, there is approach to a car park. In winter a gate in the lane leading for a further 400 yards down to another car park and a gap to the beach, is usually open. In summer however it is kept closed to cut down the number of vehicles and visitors likely to damage the marram hills and help the sea in its scouring damage. Once through this gap, the angler will often find the area to the right well built up, and good fishing is again a possibility.

Again, the last three hours of the flood, preferably in darkness, are considered best. A feature, and an extra hazard, of Horsey, is the blue black clay, locally known as ' ooze ' which is occasionally uncovered when sand has been scoured away. Leads which sink into it are difficult to regain, and much tackle is lost. Fishing is notably poor when the ooze is evident.

Apart from the thornbacks, the beach fishes moderately well for other species, especially codling in the spring, with dabs and dogfish (in summer) also being caught in numbers now and again. Longliners operate in the area and do well with thornbacks.

BOAT FISHING. Very little is done here, and again the deadly sandbanks offshore are the main reason. Dinghy anglers who persevere get good catches, but yet again it is necessary for me to remind the visitor to tread very warily, and seek local advice first.

BAIT. A few lug can be dug at low tide during springs, and brown shrimp is available from the draughtway to the angler who uses a push net.

BAIT SUPPLY AND TACKLE. As for other beaches in the area.

SOMERTON HOMES. South of Horsey, which is itself quite wild, the remote beach of Somerton Homes is as yet undefiled by commercial development. Access is difficult. A road leaves the B1159 just past the telephone kiosk (right) and Somerton memorial in the village of Somerton, but it is permanently blocked by two gates, one near the turning (left) from the B1159, and another 500 yards from the beach, which is in all about one and a half miles from the village. Access is possible on foot, bicycle or moped, but by car only with the permission and keys which must be obtained from Mr. Walter Baynes, gamekeeper of Burnley Hall Estate, nearby. Access is by no means certain, since the road is kept in repair mainly for the use of private farm vehicles. If permission is gained to take a car down, there is ample room for parking.

The beach is not heavily populated at any time, and is only lightly fished. Flanked by marram hills and dry grass and bracken, there is a real fire risk, and irresponsible behaviour would lead, undoubtedly, to no further right of access at all.

The beach is one of shingle and some sand, shelving gradually and punctuated with large stones. The most productive part of the beach is reckoned to be in the four or five groynes to the left of the access, i.e. towards Horsey. Some lug is diggable at low springs, and shrimp can be gathered with a push net. Thornbacks are taken at times, together with some good bags of dabs and flounders, and the usual sprinkling of other local species.

Dinghy access is out of the question.

WINTERTON is another commercially undefiled beach, and though access is easier than at Somerton, the locals are concerned, rightly, that it should remain so. The B1159 leads to Winterton Church, and a road from there leads half a mile down to the beach, where there is a car park. The beach shelves gradually, and is of sand and shingle, with sand at low water. The area to the north of the access gap is generally reckoned to fish better. Some thornbacks are again taken, usually at night in September, and other catches are normal for the area, though daytime fishing in summer is virtually a waste of time. There is access for dinghies, and in addition a small fleet of boats belong to local longshoremen is drawn up.

Some 200 yards to the right of the access gap, the offshore sand bar actually meets the beach, and fishing is done in the lee of the ' Point' where beach and bar meet, according to the tidal direction. Primarily an autumn and winter beach, with codling and whiting and dabs the main prospect.

H.M. Coastguard. Tel: Winterton 232 (not always manned).

HEMSBY and NEWPORT. A much more heavily populated stretch of sandy beach lies south of Winterton, between the villages of Hemsby and Newport. The only public access points are at Hemsby Gap and Newport Beach, and both are clearly sign-posted from the B1159. Again this is essentially an autumn and winter venue, with the usual good sport to be had with whiting, cod and dabs. With the sandbank offshore creating shallow water, the most productive time is the last three hours of the flood. Access for dinghies is available at Hemsby Gap, but not down the cliff entrance at Newport. Offshore fishing is quite good in Hemsby Hole, especially in May and September, when thornbacks are taken. Draw netting and beach lining is carried out by local professional fishermen, for sea trout and other species. The bank lines are thoughtfully marked by hurricane lamps or stakes, and anglers have cause to be thankful for the fact that they can recognise them and avoid loss of tackle.

The Chaney brothers, local fishermen, are famous for their method of longlining. With an offshore wind, they fly a large kite out to sea, which carries beneath it a longline baited with many hooks. When the correct distance out to sea is reached, the line is severely jerked and a weak link is broken, whereupon the line falls into the sea, to be retrieved at leisure from its shoreward anchored end!

CALIFORNIA and SCRATBY. These two holiday villages, some five miles north of Yarmouth, are again reached from the B1159. Separate signposted roads lead to each village, and there are parking facilities available. An autumn and winter stretch of beach, rather narrower than others locally, and backed by high cliffs, the fishing is well up to average as far as cod are concerned. The best fishing spots are generally considered to be north of Scratby access, and south of California slipway, just short of the beacons and exposed groynes. Best time to fish is again the last three hours of the flooding tide. A few local longlining boats are drawn up, and there is dinghy access in both villages, via slipways. The shallow beach can be very tricky during an onshore wind, and calm conditions are desirable for launch and return of small boats. As with all the beaches in this area and north, normal beach tackle is suitable, and grip leads up to six ounces are needed.

5. Great Yarmouth and Gorleston

GREAT YARMOUTH. (CHART NO. 5)

Tides: −2hr 1min from H.W. Dover, or −5hr 1min from H.W. London Bridge.

With fishing of a good standard available from beach, pier, harbour and boats, the sea angler is well catered for at Great Yarmouth. Winter results far exceed those of summer, with whiting and cod the main attraction, but the angler interested in quiet relaxation as well as heavy bags will find some fishing away from the crowds throughout the year if he cares to look for it away from the sea front. The presence of offshore 'shoals' (sandbanks) has a considerable effect upon the fishing, causing strong tides inshore, and boat hazards offshore.

CAISTER-ON-SEA. South of California, and almost into Yarmouth itself, the beach named by the seaside resort at Caister is worthy of note. It is, like all the others in the area, essentially a winter beach, and is moderately heavily fished by anglers who regard it as part of the fishing of the Yarmouth area. Only a short journey along the A149 north from Yarmouth is necessary to reach it, and access to within fifty yards is possible in at least two places. Summer parking can be a problem, of course, but in any case the holiday throng make daytime beach fishing an impractical proposition.

The beach is sandy North of the Lifeboat Shed, but South of it, the bottom is hard and well scoured. The presence offshore of the Caister Shoal, known locally as 'The Barbers' causes tides to be squeezed between the banks and the shore, with a corresponding increase in pace. At the southern end, at its strongest, the tide can throw a pound of lead back on to the beach, but fishing either side of the peak strength produces many good catches of cod and whiting. The whole stretch, and especially between Caister lifeboat shed and the coastguard lookout, which is virtually upon Yarmouth North Beach, produces good catches of cod, whiting and dabs in season.

Evidence of the tide strength can be clearly seen in the shape of turbulent water further south, off Yarmouth Point. This is locally named 'The Snickums' and is a hazard as far as small boats are concerned. Fish on the lee side according to tide direction.

57

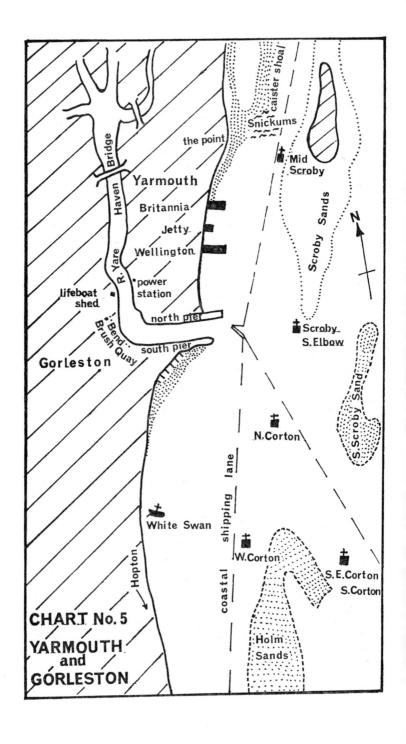

CHART No. 5
YARMOUTH
and
GORLESTON

NORTH BEACH Gt. Yarmouth. Access to this beach is easy at several points, and the beach is among the best of the local selection. As well as the cod and whiting fishing of autumn and winter, good bags of dabs and some dogfish are taken, but in the height of the holiday season, beach fishing is a waste of time, often impossible. Night fishing for the limited quantity of fish present in summer is probably not worth the effort.

The beach is again gradually shelving and sandy, and tides can be strong. Many anglers use the beach in winter, and several matches are held there, organised by the many small clubes in existence as well as the bigger ones, who sometimes hold 'open' events. No bait is available from this beach, but the local supply is adequate, and dealers are listed later.

The stretch opposite Sandown Road at the end of Marine Parade North, is universally popular, and Mr. Tovell and Mr. Coleman of Yarmouth, have taken many excellent bags of cod from opposite the 'Iron Duke' public house. Britannia Pier, covered later, marks the southern end of North Beach.

SOUTH BEACH. The beach between Britannia and Wellington piers is not bothered with by local anglers, and the next fishing of significance is that south of the Wellington. South beach stretches from here down to the North Pier of Yarmouth Harbour, and offers winter fishing well up to the average for the area. Good bags of dabs are taken from the groynes at the southern end of the beach, and further north, some 200 yards south of Wellington Pier, another local 'hotspot' is opposite the 'Green Shelter,' and from there down to the scenic railway. Towards the southern extremity of the beach, in the vicinity of the power station outlet and the harbour approaches, the water is shallow on the ebb, and the beach is not highly regarded.

As well as excellent autumn and winter fishing for cod and whiting, the beach yields the occasional bass to 7 or 8lb, and a fish of 13lb was taken some years ago.

Access to the beach is possible at many points, and though summer parking can be a problem, there is none in winter, even with the fishing at its best.

YARMOUTH HARBOUR. The great asset of the harbour is that the walls and wharves offer sheltered fishing in winter when seas outside are too rough to handle from the open beaches. In addition, the harbour offers fish of one kind or another at almost any time of the year, and though individual fish may not be big, there is ample prospect for the addict who wishes to get away from the summer crowds and fish. Eel and flounder fishing can be extremely good for some distance up river, with dabs, soles, a few school bass, excellent cod and whiting all to be taken in their seasons.

Fishing on the north side of the harbour begins on the short extension known as the North Pier. Here, at night especially, cod to 20lb, plus many smaller fish are taken in season. Good bags of the other species are also made. Within the harbour, tides are still strong and normal beach gear, even to the extent of grip leads, is often needed. Good fishing is to be had from the Freshing Houses Wharf, on past the power station (Hartman Road) and right up to the Birds-Eye factory quay. Occasional codling are taken as far upriver as this, though they are rarely big. Eels and flounders now predominate, and not surprisingly the flounders wax fat on a diet of frozen peas. The area opposite the Fish Wharf also produces good flounders, in fact Southgates Road area is generally good. Flounder fishing of very high quality extends further up river, and many good fish to near the 3lb mark are taken in the Haven Bridge area. Eels sometimes fish particularly well in the approaches to the junction of Breydon Water and the River Bure.

On the south side of the harbour, Gorleston Pier is worth fishing on the harbour and seaward side, and good bags are again to be had, especially in winter. The south side of the pier is not productive, as the water is shallow and slack. In the harbour, however, some good soles are taken at night in the warmer months from ' The Bend ' in the Brush Quay stretch. Further upriver the lifeboat station and the stretch opposite Baker Street produce good catches of codling and whiting as well as flounders, eels and dabs. Flounders and eels may be taken, as on the north side of the harbour, well up to the Haven Bridge area and beyond.

Yarmouth Piers

BRITANNIA PIER. (Situated on Marine Parade, opposite Regent Road.)

During the colder months of the whiting and cod seasons, the Britannia Pier is very popular with local and visiting anglers alike, and the fishing is very good. Many cod of over ten pounds and approaching twenty are taken, as well as dabs, flounders and good bags of whiting. In the summer months, as with local beaches, fishing is only fair, though dabs, eels, flounders, small plaice, pollack and coalfish can be taken.

Night fishing is no longer allowed on the pier, it having been closed to anglers after dusk, due to vandalism in the amusement arcade at the beach end. Between dawn and dusk throughout the year, however, the current angling charge is 1s. per rod.

The pier has an upper and lower deck, and fishing from the end of the lower deck enables the angler to start about a hundred yards beyond the normal high water mark into the deep water.

Tides, especially the flood, are strong. The flooding tide is, as described earlier in Caister Beach notes, forced between the shoreline and Caister Shoal with a resulting increase in power, and the close piling of this pier meets the full force of it, deflecting it seawards again.

The fishing area, especially on the north side, is well scoured therefore, with a bottom of clay and some settling of sand during periods of neap tide. Locals combat the strong tides with spiked leads of around 8oz and up to 12oz on occasions, fishing into the tide, letting out slack line and causing the lead to hold in much the same way as a boat's anchor. The ebb is less fierce, and lead can be reduced accordingly. The favourite spot would seem to be the N.E. corner, but the whole of the fishable area produces good catches. Most local anglers stick to the one, two or three-boomed paternoster, or a single boom with a long flowing trace. Baits are as for local beaches with lugworm by far the most popular and successful choice.

THE JETTY. This free pier, open to anglers day and night throughout the year, is situated between the Britannia and Wellington piers. A pump house on the end of it restricts casting, but there is always about forty yards of water behind the angler, more at high water, and it is a popular winter venue. An electric light provides aid for winter night anglers, who do well with cod, and whiting and dabs fish well in the autumn. Summer fishing is only fair, with crabs a nuisance and catches made up of eels, small pouting, pollack, coalfish, dabs, etc. Grip leads up to 6oz will be found ample. Baits and tackle as for local beaches.

Slipways are provided for small boats adjacent to the jetty, and trailed boats can be launched between here and Wellington Pier.

WELLINGTON PIER. This large pier offers good winter and autumn fishing for local anglers, and accommodation is available at the seaward end for thirty in comfort, more as long as everyone can cast straight! Catches are similar to those from local beaches, and normal tackle, with leads up to 6oz grip, are used.

The pier is open day and night throughout the period from October to the last week in May. There is good shelter at the seaward end, and again a light provides illumination for night anglers. The end of the pier is about forty yards beyond the low water mark, and there is ample room for casting. The cost per rod is currently 1s per day.

SMALL BOATS. There are slipways provided for small boats between the Wellington and Yarmouth Harbour.

TACKLE AND BAIT. Yarmouth:
F. Pownall, Regent Road, Great Yarmouth. Tel: 2873. Mr.

Markham, South Market Road, Great Yarmouth. Tel: 2346. Mr. Bob Davis, South Market Road, Mr. Flaxman, 23 Northgate Street. Tel: 2922. Mr. L. Bean, 124 King Street, Gt. Yarmouth. Tel: 4496.

BAITS. Lug is again the local favourite, especially for cod, whiting and dabs. Herring and fresh mackerel are used as well for the latter, and also for thornbacks, tope and dogfish from the boats. Crab is good for eels, and, of course, cod, and earthworms take fine eels in the tidal parts of the river and harbour. Harbour rag is excellent for flounders, king rag being sometimes successful, and good for cod. Shrimp is not used much by local anglers, though it is always trying both this bait and sprats in season for cod and whiting.

LOCAL EXPERTS. Fred Williams, who lives at Ordnance Road, Yarmouth, is a first rate beach angler with an intimate knowledge of local, and many other, beaches. He will be pleased to pass on information to enquiring anglers, though those who write to him must naturally restrict their queries to essential points, and enclose s.a.e. for reply.

GORLESTON BEACH.   South of Yarmouth, and separated only by the harbour, lies the town of Gorleston. For a short stretch south of the harbour, fishing in the shallow bay is only occasionally worth while, though long casters such as Ted Bean, the well-known Lowestoft tackle dealer, have occasionally taken bags of flounders.

For the next half to three-quarters of a mile the beach fishes up to the average for the area, and thereafter is generally reckoned to be of a good standard all round. The visible wreck of the White Swan lying just offshore is an easy marker. For a couple of hundred yards before this is reached, and all the way then down to Hopton, the fishing is good.

Gorleston beach is for the most part on the shallow side, with the promenade, which ends shortly before the White Swan wreck is reached, gradually giving way to low and crumbling cliff.

Access within the town is easy, and there is parking space as well as a car park in the vicinity of Bridge Road. In winter a removable post blocking access to the promenade is removed when the beaches are deserted by all except anglers, and as long as the post is replaced by drivers on the way out, there would appear to be no objection to anglers parking along the prom itself. This facility is certainly not available in summer, however.

Coming south, there is a road along the top of the cliffs which eventually ends, and thereafter the angler will have to walk if he wishes to fish still further south. The quickest access to the White Swan area is to leave Gorleston on the A12, turning off left down Links Lane which gives access to the beach.

Again it is the winter cod and autumn whiting which fish best, but this beach is good for dabs, dogfish, eels and flounders in their respective seasons. The beach is fairly shallow, there is not much distance between high and low water marks, and tides can be strong enough to demand grip leads on occasions. In general the flood is more productive. Though just as good as other beaches in the area, it is not as heavily fished as those within walking distance of the many sea anglers in Yarmouth.

TACKLE DEALERS. Bait, tackle and advice can be obtained from Baker and O'Keefe, 7 Pier Walk, Gorleston. Tel: Gt. Yarmouth 62448; and Edwards, 16 Quayside, Gorleston. Tel: Gt. Yarmouth 61095. Bait must be ordered in advance.

Great Yarmouth Area

BOAT FISHING. As has already been explained, the sandbanks or 'shoals' lying offshore in the Yarmouth area have an effect upon tides and fishing conditions as far as beach fishing is concerned. From the boat fishing point of view they are even more significant, since the banks themselves are more of a hazard to the unwary, and the tidal run in places makes fishing impossible. These points will be enlarged upon later.

LARGE BOATS. Though there are many suitable craft in use by longshoremen, trawlermen and longliners, no one, to my knowledge, operates a full-time service for party angling. Nevertheless, it is possible for the visiting angler to arrange boat fishing as long as he is perpared to make arrangements well in advance. Since it is not economical for the single angler to pay the full hire of a boat, it is far better for parties to make group bookings. There are no boats waiting at the quayside to take out whoever comes along, and there is therefore little chance of the visitor turning up in the hope that he can 'make up the number' for the day.

Should a party of friends wish to go out from Yarmouth, however, Mr. Frank Moore, of Taunton House, 9 Nelson Road South, Gt. Yarmouth, is the man to contact. Mr. Moore is a professional fisherman, and is secretary of the Great Yarmouth and District Inshore Fishermen and Beachmen's Federation. In this capacity he is willing and able to put visiting anglers in touch with those professionals like himself who are, from time to time, prepared to take out anglers for rod and line angling.

At weekends in the height of the whiting and cod seasons, as many as thirty boats might be available, most of them around twenty-two-and-a-half feet in length, and capable of taking up to six anglers. The normal charge is £6 per boat, and place and time of departure must be arranged by post beforehand. During the week, many boat owners are working in other capacities and are not available, but a few are, and fishing is a possibility.

The angler is advised to contact Mr. Moore at least a month in advance, especially for winter fishing when the demand is great. The pattern which naturally develops when boats are in short supply is for visiting parties to re-book for the coming season as a means of making certain of a boat, and 'regulars' naturally appreciate the wisdom of these early arrangements. October, though excellent for cod fishing, is likely to find most of these boats in use for longshore work which is the boatman's main source of income, and the chances of finding a man willing to take out parties is reduced.

As a general rule, once the boat is booked, fishing time will be from about 8 a.m. to 4 p.m., but alternative arrangements are possible. Boats can leave Yarmouth Harbour at any stage of the tide, and the Town Hall on the Yarmouth side, the lifeboat shed on the Gorleston side, are popular picking-up points. With almost no exceptions, the areas fished by the larger boats are the same as those applicable to smaller craft. Details will be supplied later.

SMALL BOATS. No one operates a dinghy hire service for visiting anglers, though enquiries may enable the occasional hiring to be arranged.

Trailed boats can be launched from Gorleston, Yarmouth and Caister beaches in many places, however, and there is good boat fishing in autumn and winter just offshore. The warnings applicable to dinghy users in other parts of the East Coast have been mentioned many times to date, and are doubly important at Yarmouth, where sandbanks or shoals lying offshore create fast tides, turbulance and, in many cases, an effective means of preventing a boat from getting back to the beach from the seaward side when weather is rough. H.M. Coastguard Tel: Gt. Yarmouth 63444.

FISHING AREAS. Taking large boats and small ones into consideration then, the outward limit of the fishing is normally the line of buoys marking the offshore shoals. (See Chart No. 5.) Very few large boats, certainly no smaller craft, go to the seaward side of these banks. In summer the boat fishing is not good, and venturing out into very strong tides and dangerous roads between the banks will not improve it. What thornbacks, dabs, eels, flounders, dogfish and occasional tope are to be taken, are all found well inside the shoals. In winter there is no need for the boat angler to fish very far offshore, and many excellent cod of over 20lb, together with huge bags of codling and whiting, are taken within easy reach of the beach.

The general area thus available under safe conditions (and with E., S.E. or N.E. winds prevailing, there is no safety for

1 The biggest cod ever caught on rod and line in a boat off the British Isles. Tony Marsh of Ipswich with his 43lb fish, taken off Felixstowe in January 1968

2 Crab, lug and squid. A good mouthful for a good cod

3 One man—many cod! John Sait of Brightlingsea poses with a one-day catch off Holland Haven. Best 32lb

4 Hazards of a
crowded pier

5 Roy Leeder of Wivenhoe with a tremendous bass of 14¾lb taken
off Felixstowe in 1968

6 "The Old Style". A Lowestoft angler with a casting stick

7 "and the new". Fred Williams of Great Yarmouth in expectant
mood

9 Used properly, "a passport to success". A small East Coast dinghy off Felixstowe

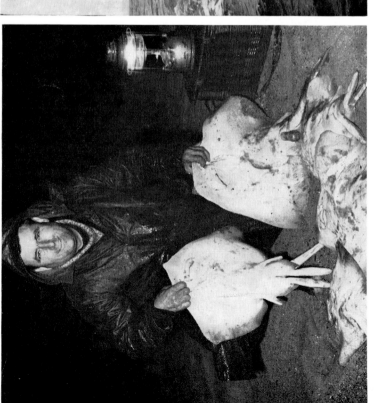

8 Fred Williams with Norfolk beach-caught thornbacks

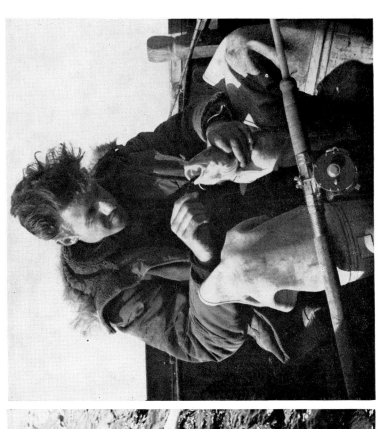

11 An average East Coast cod

10 A 12lb thornback comes to the gaff

12 Mr A. Woolhouse with a plaice of nearly 4lb taken from Cromer Pier

small craft) is a big one, extending both north and south of Yarmouth Harbour parallel to the shore. In winter, when the fishing is at its best, boats half a mile or so offshore will do well enough, and the larger craft sometimes extend this to one and a half miles. Outside that, the area is definitely not safe.

There are few marks which can be said to fish better for cod or whiting than any others, though the area on either side of the harbour entrance is popular for those species and good dabs as well. The occasional big tope (Mr. Heard of Yarmouth had one of over 30lb as well as a stingray of similar size on the same day in 1963) and other summer species are all taken in this inshore area, and anywhere between the S. Caister buoy (which marks turbulence known locally as ' The Snickums ') north of Yarmouth, and a similar stretch south is likely to produce catches in winter, and summer alike which are as good as any other spot. Most local boats fish in the area between the White Swan wreck off Gorleston beach, and the power station outfall near Nelson's Monument, a mile north of the harbour.

TACKLE and BAITS. Normal boat tackle will be found adequate at Yarmouth, though leads up to a pound in weight, heavier than in many places elsewhere on this coast, may be needed. As with Britannia Pier anglers, many local boat fishermen prefer to cast up tide with very heavy leads and pay out line so that a spiked lead will ' anchor ' on the bottom in the same way as the boat's anchor does. The visitor who is used to fishing down tide may like to compare both methods.

Lugworm is the almost universally successful bait, though the others used in this area, such as peeler crab, herring strip, squid, king rag, etc., will all take fish. Mackerel are sometimes to be taken on feathers during the summer, and fresh herring can be obtained in spring and autumn from longshoremen. Sprats are often excellent for whiting, sometimes cod as well.

TACKLE DEALERS. As for those mentioned in beach notes for Yarmouth.

LOCAL ADVICE. Mr. Frank Moore will be pleased to give help and advice to the visitor who inquires, and useful information may be gained by asking politely in the Inshore Fishermens Rest Room, which is open at weekends and on most evenings, and which is situated in Marine Parade near the jetty. (Between the piers.)

ACCOMMODATION. There is a great deal of accommodation available in this large seaside resort, but in view of the situation concerning large boats and the difficulty of booking them at peak times, it may be of interest to mention that Frank Moore will arrange winter accommodation for parties of anglers who wish to spend a few days boat fishing for cod or whiting.

E

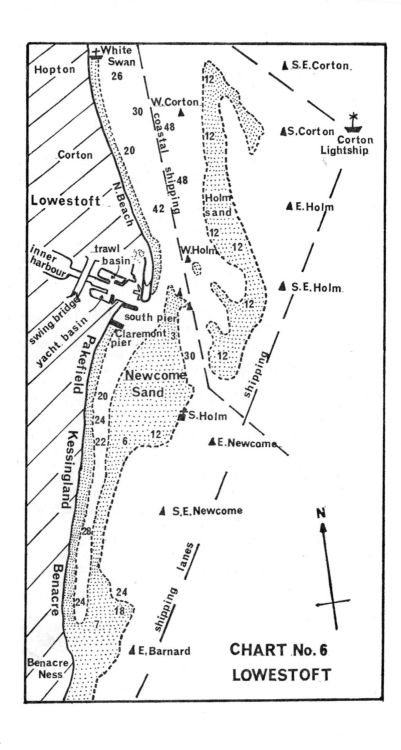

CHART No. 6
LOWESTOFT

6. The Suffolk Coast

LOWESTOFT (Suffolk). (CHART NO. 6)

Tides: —4hrs 26min from H.W. London Bridge.

LOWESTOFT NESS is the most easterly point in the British Isles, and the town itself is a very busy commercial fishing port, from which a large fleet of drifters and trawlers operates. Much of the livelihood of the town centres around commercial fishing, and summer tourism. The angler and his family will find a great deal to interest them in the thriving fish market, to which the boats bring herrings, mackerel, cod and flatfish in vast quantities.

Sea fishing in and around Lowestoft is carried on from a number of beaches, two piers, harbour walls, and from boats offshore. Summer beach fishing is sometimes out of the question for Lowestoft attracts vast numbers of summer holiday makers, both on its own account, and through its close connection with Broadland. The beaches are wonderful for bathing, and the older part of the town, with its narrow streets and old buildings are a big attraction. Lowestoft is about 100 miles N.E. of London.

SHORE FISHING. There are several beaches in the area, which do not alter greatly in character, and all of which produce broadly similar sport. As with most East Coast fishing, cod and whiting in the autumn and winter months are the main attraction to the sea angler, but a variety of other species can be taken at other times of the year.

Access to these beaches is easy at most points, but permission has to be sought on occasions in order to pass through caravan or holiday camps. Parking charges may be levied in the holiday season, and in the winter months when the cod are running, the week-end angler may have a few minutes walking to do along a cliff-top footpath in order to find a spot clear of other anglers. Access is, in the main, via one of the many side roads leading from the main A12.

Generally speaking, conventional beach tackle, with grip leads up to six ounces, and paternoster or trace end gear, is used.

Lowestoft is the home of one of the most well-known beach anglers in the British Isles. Sam Hook, who owns a tackle shop in Bevan Street, held the cod record with a 32lb fish, taken from the Claremont Pier in 1945, for twenty years. He has, in addition taken thousands of other good fish from many spots along this coast, and is a mine of useful information. Ted Bean is another local tackle dealer who will put a great deal of practical experience at the disposal of the visiting angler, all of which can be relied upon as accurate and helpful.

HOPTON. This beach, and the village which gives it its name, lies some four miles to the north of Lowestoft. At the time of writing there are no restricted areas, and a long, more or less straight, stretch of shallow and sandy beach is available to the angler. The beach is perfectly safe for angling and bathing.

Tidal strength is not great except on springs, and fishing without grip leads is often possible. No bait can be gathered here, which means that the angler will need to order in advance. Lug is the most popular choice, especially before and after Christmas, when the beach has a reputation for its cod fishing. Whiting fish well there in autumn, and as well as lug, fish strip baits will then prove successful. Dabs are often plentiful in the spring, but neither thornbacks nor mackerel are caught with any kind of regularity.

Species which are caught, though none with the frequency of the cod in its season, include flounders, and dogfish in the autumn, plus the occasional tope, whilst silver eels, soles, smelt, the occasional bass, brill and turbot turn up in June/July. It would be a mistake to rely upon catching any of the occasional visiting species, however. Other baits used include king rag and small rag for flats, fish baits (especially when available fresh from Lowestoft) for tope and dogs, and soft crab for all species, if one can get hold of it. Eels in particular love soft crab, but it is not easily obtainable, though tackle shops do supply it sometimes. Although lugworm is the standard bait in winter, mussel is always worth trying for cod.

Since it produces, on the whole, good average fishing, Hopton is fairly heavily fished. Night fishing on most East Anglian beaches is almost always more productive, especially when the tides are right, and these beaches near Lowestoft are no exception.

The occasional 'Open Match' is fished here by local clubs, mostly in the spring. There is generally plenty of room for many anglers, except when holiday crowds throng the beach.

Local opinion has it that the area to the north of the coast-guard lookout point is the most productive one. Mr. A. Bullent, of the Corton White Horse, can be approached for more precise information.

Winter anglers like to see a little chop on the water whilst cod fishing, and even in rough seas, sport does not deteriorate. With E. or N.E. onshore winds above force four, however, it becomes very difficult to hold even with the heaviest lead. There are many local anglers along the length of this coast who maintain that easterly winds have some particular feature which puts fish off feed, but my own opinion is that the sheer physical difficulty of fishing at all in a heavy undertow or mammoth surf created by strong easterlies is the main cause of poor catches. For other species of course, somewhat calmer seas are preferred.

CORTON. A mile or so nearer to Lowestoft lies the village of Corton, and once again there is reasonable beach fishing within easy reach. Conditions, species caught and baits applicable are precisely as for Hopton. ' Tramps Alley ' is the local ' hot ' spot for cod in the season, and since tidal strengths are perceptably stronger, grip leads will be useful.

NORTH BEACH LOWESTOFT. Within half a mile of Lowestoft itself, North Beach offers good sea fishing. Again it is principally cod, whiting and dab fishing, with the November cod fishing being particularly good. Access to the beach is easy and for the most part free parking, though in the summer months, a car park must be used for access to the north end of the beach.

The beach is safe, though half a mile due south at Ness Point there is a danger of being cut off by rising tides.

The best fishing is reckoned to be had anywhere between Lowestoft Highlight and the north boundary at the end of North Parade and the sea wall. The remarks concerning other local beaches as far as species, bait and tackle are involved, continue to be applicable.

The beach is very heavily fished in the autumn, when both cod and whiting abound, and matches are held there by the local clubs. ' Open ' matches sometimes take place in the spring, and, taken all round, this is one of the most productive and favoured local beaches.

PAKEFIELD. A mile south of Lowestoft, another excellent beach is available to the angler at Pakefield. Access is via the roads leaving the A12, and if the private ones leading down through Pontins Holiday Camp or Cliftonville Camping Site are chosen, permission to cross will need to be obtained. In the built up area of Pakefield itself, access can be gained via All Saints Road, and one will be in line with the last of the breakwaters and groynes immediately to the south of Lowestoft.

Like North Beach, Pakefield is very popular, since it gives good all-round results. Cod to 27lb have been taken here, as well as very heavy bags of smaller fish, together with whiting and dabs in season. Grip leads are standard, especially if the beach is being fished by others nearby, and tides run quite strongly. The ebb is reckoned to produce marginally better catches, and night fishing in winter is, as always, very worthwhile. Stretches opposite the holiday camps mentioned, together with those opposite Pakefield Church and Harbour Lane, are well known locally as good spots.

Tackle, bait and general species, as for other beaches in this area.

Pakefield is the beach used by the organisers of the annual

Lowestoft Sea Angling Festival, held at the end of October, and also for the Cliftonville Charity Match, which is held at the beginning of the same month. Many other local club matches are also held here throughout the season.

Pakefield is an attractive beach from all points of view. At the base of the cliffs (along which it will be necessary to walk to find a free spot when the fish are about) there is a wide strip of low dunes and sea grass upon which holiday makers enjoy themselves. Though summer catches do not normally involve the weighty bags taken when the cod are about, the early and late summer produce many a grand day, when fish are feeding and plenty of flats plus the odd codling can be taken by the angler whose family are also enjoying the off-peak freedom of the dunes. As the tourist season gets under way, the beach angler generally looks elsewhere in the daylight hours.

KESSINGLAND. Leaving Pakefield beach, and some five miles south of Lowestoft, another favourite stretch of coast is that at Kessingland. Popular with holiday makers in summer, the beach is also recognised as a good average one for beach fishing. It is very similar in character to the other local beaches, and the general details for those apply equally well here. Cod well in excess of 20lb have been taken, and a good spot for cod, particularly in the favourite month of November, is that opposite the Kessingland Sailors' Home.

If it is at all possible, it is worth looking around at low tide to locate obstructions which appear from time to time and which could foul tackle. There is occasionally a floating weed problem when S.W. winds prevail on the ebb tide.

During the ebb, long casting will give the best results, but the period just before top water is very productive during the cod and whiting seasons. Access to the beach is easy at most points, and little walking is involved from the car in many places. The beach is fairly well fished, and results are well up to the local average.

BENACRE. This beach lies on the southern fringe of the Lowestoft area, and is different in character from those further north. There is much deeper water, fished from a steeply shelving sand and shingle ridge beach. Access is limited to the narrow lane leaving the A12 at Walnut Tree corner in Benacre. Turning and parking space is restricted, and cars should be left away from the lane. A walk of a quarter of a mile or so will then be necessary to reach the beach.

Species and baits are similar to other local beaches, but the chance of a thornback on the rising tide in June, especially at night, is more likely here.

South of Benacre Ness, the beach, though straight enough, runs more to the west, and is therefore slightly more susceptible to

S. and S.E. winds, as well as the easterlies. Anything over force
four from these directions makes fishing difficult. There is also
something of a weed problem at times after prolonged N.W. winds,
and this is at its worst at around half ebb.

Benacre is best known for its autumn and winter fishing, for
cod and whiting, with the chance of a thornback in spring, and
some fishing for flats in season. Due to the limited access it is
less fished and less visited than other local beaches.

BOAT FISHING.   Though Lowestoft is first and foremost a fishing port, and a thriving one, there is not what one would describe
as a smoothly organised hiring service available to the rod and
line angler. The general procedure is for anglers wishing to go
out in small parties to contact the local tackle dealers, and to be
put in touch then with the boatmen who do operate, some on a
full-time basis, for the benefit of anglers.

Once this has been accomplished, hiring fees, departure times,
etc., are settled by individual arrangement, and in many cases
regular contact between parties and boatmen is established. One or
two addresses which will to a certain extent shorten this procedure are given at the end of this chapter. No dinghies are available for hire, and in view of the changeable nature of the weather
and the busy boat traffic, it is not advisable to go to sea in a
trailed dinghy without first obtaining a great deal of local advice.
Dinghies can be launched from the beaches already covered, but
surf conditions often demand the experience gained through
having done plenty of small boat fishing on a coast of this type.

Having said that, I will qualify it to an extent by pointing out
that the experienced dinghy fisherman will find good fishing, when
weather permits the use of his small boat, often within half a
mile of the shore.

The general remarks made at the beginning of this book concerning the results from boats compared with beach apply at
Lowestoft. The fishing is, broadly speaking, for the same species,
but the catches very much heavier. In addition, the thornback
ray, the tope and the mackerel are much more readily caught
from boats. Many thornbacks, or 'roker' as they are called
locally, to 20lb are landed. Tope to 56lb have been taken, but
the tope fishing is not as yet fully explored. Bags of cod in excess
of a hundredweight per rod are not unknown, and very big cod,
in excess of 20lb, are taken every year. Local anglers Sam Hook,
Jack Colby, Brian Mumford, Bob Williams and Colin Humphreys
have all taken many double figure cod and extremely heavy bags
of fish from the popular marks, as indeed have most knowledgeable local boat anglers.

A glance at the Admiralty Chart for the area (No. 1504) reveals
that there is a complex and heavily buoyed system of channels
and sandbanks out from Lowestoft Harbour, and though the

regular visitor could in time, gain enough local knowledge to explore the fishing from his own boat, one is wisest to begin by sampling the fishing from a bigger local craft, with the guidance of a local boatman. The simplified diagram included here, gives some idea of depths and local features, but it is in no way adequate for navigational purposes.

Popular marks for cod, whiting, thornbacks and tope include the areas around the N.E. Newcome, East N.E. Newcome, S.E. Barnard, and Ness Point Light buoys. With the exception of the N.E. Newcome on a fine day, these marks are three to five miles out from the harbour, and are out of reach of the casual dinghy angler.

Normal boat tackle, that is to say for the smaller species a light boat outfit, and for the heavier ones a medium outfit, will be perfectly adequate. Leads up to a pound in weight are needed on the outer marks, and half that is general. Naturally, when tides are slacker, or one is inshore, less lead can sometimes be used for the bottom feeding varieties. For average boatwork, a rod suited to a 20lb line and 6 to 8oz lead will be found excellent for use with everything apart from big tope and the heaviest of cod.

BOATMEN. At the time of writing, the following boatmen, all reliable, may be approached. If writing, please enclose a stamped addressed envelope for a reply. The boatmen take parties of four anglers, primarily for cod and whiting in winter, thornbacks and general species in summer, to marks offshore. Tackle is not provided, neither is bait, but hot tea is available on board in each case. Fees and departure times are by individual arrangement.

Bob Williams of Whitby House, Lowestoft, operates from the Yacht Basin in 'Andy Billy', and Mr. Arthur Rudd, North Parade, Lowestoft, keeps 'Corinthia' at Kirby Marine. R. Fuller, 49 Avondale Road, Lowestoft, has a 26 ft. diesel available. These boats are available at all times throughout the year, and all are reliable craft. H.M. Coastguard: Tel. Lowestoft 5365.

Lowestoft Piers

SOUTH PIER. Situated near the swing bridge in the centre of the town, the South Pier is a safe one for youngsters, and fishes quite well in winter for cod and whiting, with fair catches of flats, too. Summer fishing is not so good, though small pollack, coalfish, smelt and eels are taken, and sometimes better catches of soles and mullett. The pier toll is 3d, and the angling charge 6d per day per rod. South Pier is controlled by the Lowestoft Corporation, and any alterations in the prevailing fishing arrangements can be clarified by the Corporation's Information Bureau. The pier is of interest to the family, and is quite safe for youngsters.

CLAREMONT PIER. This Lowestoft pier is famous as the origin of Sam Hook's 32lb British record cod, taken from the celebrated 'cod corner' on November 12, 1945, and which stood for twenty years. Again the fishing in winter for cod and whiting is the major activity, and Mr. Rose, the pier owner, allows the last of the cod to disappear before he closes it altogether for annual overhaul. It opens again for the tourist season, at the end of which the cod re-appear. Summer fishing does produce a variety of species, mostly flats, but not in outstanding quantity by the highest of angling standards. Nevertheless, catches of soles, plaice, the occasional turbot and isolated bass do make interesting results possible, if not a certainty.

The fishing charge is currently 1s per rod per day, and the pier, which is about 400 feet long, is open daily from 8.30 a.m. until 5 p.m. A large number of anglers, well over 200, can be accommodated on the upper deck. The local clubs are sometimes given extended fishing hours in the evenings during the cod season.

The tendency these days is for anglers to use beachcasting rods for pier work as well, rather than obtain the familiar shorter rod favoured in the past for pier fishing. Both will be perfectly adequate here, and paternoster tackle is popular. A single hook on a long trace will be a better cod outfit, especially in November, when really big fish are very much a prospect. Grip leads of 6 and 8oz will be needed according to the state of the tide. Baits are as for local beaches.

TACKLE DEALERS. Sam Hook, 132 Bevan Street, Lowestoft. Ted Bean, 175 London Road North, Lowestoft.

Both these dealers are extremely well known sea anglers, who will not only advise upon choice of tackle and arrange supplies of bait, but can also be relied upon to give an accurate assessment of current prospects and likely areas.

COVEHITHE. Leaving the A12 at Wrentham, the angler can drive down to the coastguard station area in the village of Cove-hithe. Parking space is limited in summer, but usually adequate in winter. Going south, this is the last access to the beach until Southwold is reached, and for that reason the stretch is not heavily fished, at least, not to the extent where the angler who is prepared to walk a distance cannot find a spot to fish. About halfway between Covehithe and Easton Bavents there is a lane leading to the beach, but this is currently private, and access is not granted. Remains of war defences can cause loss of tackle in the Easton Bavents area, but this is localised.

North of Covehithe the background to the beach is flat, but south there are cliffs stretching along to Southwold itself. The beach everywhere is shingle and sand, fairly shallow, and without

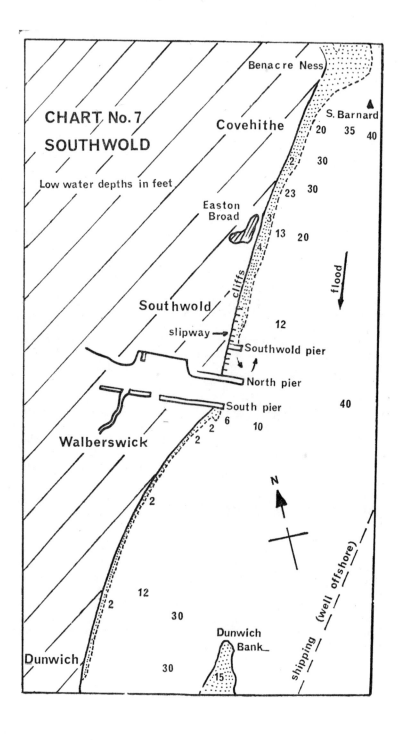

terribly strong tides. The accent is on winter fishing, though flats and eels can produce good bags at times in summer.

SOUTHWOLD. (CHART NO. 7)

Tides: −3hrs 51min from H.W. London Bridge.

This fairly large town is situated on a reasonably clear stretch of beach which gives good fishing, principally in winter. Summer fishing is not often greatly productive, but would be if the boat fishing was more developed. Boats are available, but as in so many places down the East Coast, it is not carried out on a highly organised and widespread scale. There is also a certain amount of lesser fishing from the Harbour walls.

SHORE FISHING. Beach fishing at Southwold is well up to the average for the coast, and the area does, in addition, boast some bass and soles which are something of a luxury. Though fairly crowded during the summer months, access to the beach in the vicinity of the town is easy, and there are car parks near the pier, plenty of parking spaces along the front, and another car park near the harbour. Charges are not made during the winter. As with all beaches, certain parts have a reputation among the locals, but in fact the whole of the beach fishes well, and cod to 20lb or so have frequently been taken. If anything, the beach to the north side of the harbour tends to fish best, due to the feed which is washed out of the harbour mouth, to collect in the eddy created by the ebb tide, which runs northerly. (The local effect is for the ebb tide to create a flow in the 'flood' direction for several hundred yards adjacent to the harbour on the north side.)

The only snaggy area is the north at Easton Bavents, which has already been mentioned. Otherwise the beaches are clear, and tides are not too strong. Leads up to five ounces maximum, with grips being useful when strong winds create heavy seas, will be more than adequate. In addition to good cod and whiting, eels plaice, flounders, the occasional shoal of mackerel, dabs, some bass and dogfish are taken by beach anglers. Some excellent mullet occupy the harbour in the warmer months, but seldom fall to rod and line. Immature mullet are taken from the Went, which is a creek leading off from the harbour slightly inland.

SOUTHWOLD PIER. This is not a long pier, and is generally regarded more as a place to fish when rough seas prevail on the beaches, rather than an exceptionally productive spot. The angling charge is currently 2s per day, and the pier closes at 5 p.m. in winter, 7 p.m. in summer. Occasionally some excellent bags of soles are taken from the pier, as well as the usual run of common

East Coast species. Use of a drop net will provide plenty of shrimp and some crab in season.

SOUTHWOLD HARBOUR.   The principal fishing of note is the bass fishing which takes place from the southern bar of the harbour entrance. Most of the fish are taken by anglers who spin with rubber sandeels, but soft and peeler crab is also effective. (A certain amount of the latter can be gathered from a rocky area on the north side of the harbour, and inland a little.) Bass are by no means a certainty, but it is always worth trying from this spot, and some heavy fish have been taken at times. The attraction is a mixture of concrete baffles and iron cagework which is a haven for crab, small fish, and other creatures upon which bass prey, coupled with a good flow through the open piles of the bar. From both sides of the harbour, which is very narrow, codling, whiting, eels and dabs, but, strangely, no flounders in recent years, can all be taken in season. As stated, there are also some difficult grey mullet to tantalise the angler. A short extension on the north side of the harbour, known as the North Pier, is also available, and it fishes similar to the beaches. Access is permanent and free, though cars are not allowed on it.

WALBERSWICK.   There are few access points along this stretch of coast, and the angler wishing to fish here must either approach from across the dunes at Walberswick itself, which involves a walk of two or three hundred yards, or walk along the beach to the next access south at Dunwich.

Fishing results are similar to those of other beaches in the area, and in addition some excellent bass are occasionally taken. One or two fish have exceeded 10lb, but it would take a persistent angler, or a lucky one, to achieve constant success. The species is not really prolific. What fish which have been taken have usually fallen for a spun rubber eel, though a strip of really fresh fish bait, squid or crab could always prove successful. The beach is fishable at all states of the tide, and tackle is as for other local beaches.

SOUTHWOLD BOATS.   Access for dinghy fishermen to launch their own boats is made via a slipway 100 yards north of the pier. Launching is possible at all stages of the tide, and no charge is made. Other points of dinghy access are close to the harbour and, if the boat is large enough to cope adequately with the tidal run at the harbour mouth, from inside the harbour at the Harbour Inn. Due to the presence of a sandbar some 150 yards offshore, running almost the length of Southwold, navigation can be very tricky, and bad winds can cause difficulty. The problems thus created have been emphasised throughout in this book, and the visitor is urged to seek local advice.

Party boats are available at Southwold, and they leave from the Harbour Inn. No small boats are available there for hire. Two reliable and well equipped boatmen are: Mr. Paddy Pile, Station Road, Southwold. Tel: Southwold 3161. He will take up to ten anglers, and the current charge for hire of the boat is £10 per day. He operates on weekdays, but is always heavily booked during the whiting and cod season, so that advance booking is essential. Bait will be supplied by previous arrangement, and the cost is additional.

Mr. Amas, 105 Church Road, Kessingland, Tel: Kessingland 416, also has a large boat available at weekends only. He will take up to eight anglers, and the charge is currently £9 per day. Time of departure, bait supply and time of return can be settled by previous arrangement. Again, early booking is necessary. Both boats are well equipped, and operate under Board of Trade licence.

Boat fishing at Southwold is not carried out with specific marks in mind, although locals have some preferences. In general though, the winter fishing in particular is very uniform. The better cod are usually found a mile or more offshore, but dinghy anglers often take heavy bags very much closer to the shore. More thornbacks fall to boat anglers in the warmer months than beach anglers ever encounter, and fresh bait in the shape of mackerel caught out at sea on feathers or spinners will obviously be a boon to the boat angler. One or two excellent tope have been taken, to around the 40lb mark, but generally speaking there is little specialisation. It is a criticism of almost all East Coast boat fishing that the abundance of cod and whiting in season, and a few thornbacks to take up the brief summer months, make for a lack of exploitation of all that the sea has to offer. The visitor will therefore, often have to find things out for himself, not just at Southwold, but all along the coast.

TACKLE AND ADVICE. Mr. C. H. Land, proprietor of the well equipped tackle shop at 13 East Street, Southwold, will be found able and willing to give advice. He is also the only supplier of lugworm for several miles in any direction. Orders must be made in advance to: C. H. Land, Fishing Tackle, 13 East Street, Southwold, Suffolk. Telephone Southwold 2085. Mr. Land also supplies Tide Tables for the area.

DUNWICH. South of Walberswick the coast turns slightly south-west into Dunwich Bay, and a long stretch of clean sand and shingle, shelving into quite deep water, provides uncrowded beach fishing for several miles. The area is visited in summer, but the lack of commercialisation and holiday facilities, compared with other places to the north and south, means that it never gets really heavily populated.

DUNWICH BAY.   Access to this three miles or so of beach is from Walberswick to the north, or the village of Dunwich to the south. The beach is quite featureless as far as angling is concerned. but is none the less beautiful for that. Winter anglers who love the solitude of a night after cod on a wild and exposed coast will find all they require, including fish, at Dunwich. A fish of over 30lb, possibly at the time a new record for the British Isles, was caught here only a year or two ago. Species are the normal ones for the area, with the accent, as usual, on night fishing in season for whiting and cod. Occasional good bags of flats are taken, and there are some very fine plaice taken by the professional longshoremen and inshore trawlers who keep their small fleet at Dunwich. Thornbacks are also encountered by these boats offshore, but cannot be expected by beach anglers.

The beach is one of shelving sand/shingle throughout its length, flanked by marram and marshland. Tackle is as for other local beaches.

BOATS.   There are none for hire at Dunwich, but there is a slipway available for the use of dinghy anglers. A very exposed coast as always, however, and one which needs to be well understood before risks are taken. There is ample car parking in winter, but this is charged for in summer, when there is a small cafe and a supply of fresh-caught fish from the longshoremen.

MINSMERE.   Cliffs start at the village of Dunwich and continue south for about two miles. These offer shelter from strong offshore winds, but the water is rather shallower some three hundred yards offshore, where a typical sand bar also begins, or rather, rises near enough to the surface to create turbulence at low water. There is deep enough water for beach fishing, however, and again the winter cod and whiting can be good. Access is from Dunwich, as for Dunwich Bay, and also slightly further south via the roal leading to the coastguard cottages. The cliffs can be crumbly and dangerous, and damage to either the cliffs or the specially planted grasses is an offence. Owing to the presence of the bar, fishing is most profitable three hours either side of high water.

BOATS.   There is no additional access for boats, but this area is within reach of those launched from the beach at Dunwich. Expert advice should be obtained from the local fishermen, however, for apart from the close-to sand bank, there is another much bigger one, Dunwich Bank, about a mile offshore which can produce turbulent and dangerous surf when unfavourable winds spring up, as they often do.

MINSMERE SLUICE.   A mile past the end of Minsmere Cliffs,

a sluice occurs, and freshwater drainage from the marches runs into the sea. This is reached either by a long walk from Dunwich, or Sizewell to the south, or again by a two mile long public footpath which starts inland in the village of East Bridge. The angler who really requires solitude will almost certainly find it there, but although the fishing is up to the average for the local beaches, there is no special reward other than peace and quiet for those prepared to make the long journey on foot! The footpath starts near the ' Eels Foot.'

SIZEWELL. About a mile and a half further south, the site of a large and modern power station at Sizewell causes anglers to think in terms of warm water attracting all sorts of unusual fish, and affecting the general standard of angling. In fact there is very little evidence to suggest that any effects have been forthcoming, and the fishing in this area is similar to that everywhere else in the immediate vicinity. There are a few cottages at the end of the road from Leiston inland, which is in turn reached via the B1119 from the A12, the junction being at Saxmundham. Beach fishing is straightforward enough, there are no real snags, though outcrops of rock make it advisable to do without grips leads and to retrieve quickly. One or two of the local fishermen may be persuaded to take out the visitor, but this cannot be guaranteed, and there are no boats for hire.

THORPENESS. Most of the beach and the town of Thorpeness is privately owned. There are no restrictions, however, parking is free throughout the year, and there is a holiday camp as well as a large boating lake to attract the holiday makers in summer. The ground is somewhat more snaggy and much shallower water exists here, with the result that the beach fishing is mediocre. Codling, whiting and flats are taken, but other beaches in the area are more productive. Summer day-time fishing is affected by holiday visitors, but one feature of night fishing is the occasional good bag of enormous soles, locally called ' grandfathers ' or ' whiskered ' soles.

ALDEBURGH.
Tides: —3hrs 8min from H.W. London Bridge.
This very attractive Suffolk town is reached by road via the B1094 which leaves the A12 just north of Farnham. Access is straightforward and there is also a coastal road leading to Thorpeness, all of which is available for parking. A car park is provided in the centre of the town to the right of the lifeboat shed, and the angler will find himself no more than a few yards from the beach. For reasons unknown to locals, the fishing is not as good opposite the town itself as it is to the south, past the solitary Martello Tower. To the north of the town fishing for flats can be very productive up to a point midway between Aldeburgh and Thorpe-

ness. Here a freshwater sluice enters the sea, marked by two
beacons, and north of this the water becomes rather shallow
and much less productive.

The favourite area is, then, to the south, where breakwaters
and obstructions end. At Slaughden beach, a mile or so south,
the river Alde, running more or less parallel to the beach, runs
very close to the sea, and fishing in either is possible. The
local ' hotspot ' for almost all species is known as the ' Dirty Wall '
and is just north of the wire fence which surrounds the Ministry
A.W.R.E. prohibited area, and which prevents further access to
the beach. This spot is one of the few places where thornbacks
are taken in season, mostly at night.

Beach fishing at Aldeburgh is into fairly deep water, and the
beach is again of shingle and sandy patches, with the greater part
of it large stones fairly steeply shelving. Opposite the town itself
and for a long way to the north, low water, especially during onshore winds, reveals the presence of the sandbar only a hundred
yards or so offshore. It never stands completely dry, but is probably
one of the main reasons for the fact that little boat fishing is carried
on here either by locals or visitors, though there is a small longshore
fleet in operation. No boats are for hire.

Aldeburgh provides good codling and whiting fishing in season,
and the town is an extremely attractive one. Other species for
the area are frequently taken in good numbers, and one local
angler worth contacting for up-to-the-minute advice, which will
be useful and freely given, is Mr. Charlie Linsell, who is secretary
of the local club. He has taken very good bags of cod to 22lb
from the ' Dirty Wall ' area, with several other fish nearing twenty
pounds. He has also had some very good nights in the same
vicinity with soles and dabs, but these are never quite so predictable
as the cod are in a good year.

TACKLE is as for most East Coast beaches, with tides increasing in strength as one moves south. Four to 6oz grip leads
are sometimes needed, but very often less will do.

BAIT. There is not a happy situation in Aldeburgh as far as
bait is concerned. The nearest source of supply for the whole
stretch south of Southwold is, in fact, tackle dealer Mr. Land
in that town, whose address has already been furnished. No
natural bait of any kind is obtainable from the beaches. Anglers
travelling from a southerly point could obtain bait, ordered in
advance, from The Anglers Tackle Shop in Woodbridge. (See
notes on Felixstowe.)

TACKLE DEALERS. There is no large tackle shop in Aldeburgh, and Southwold and Woodbridge are the sources for major
items. Local angler Mr. F. Eade is the proprietor of a cycle and

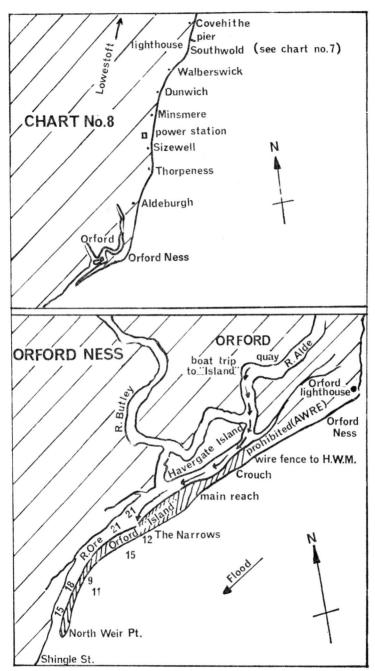

CHART No.8

Covehithe
pier
Southwold (see chart no.7)

lighthouse

Lowestoft

Walberswick

Dunwich

Minsmere

power station

Sizewell

Thorpeness

N

Aldeburgh

Orford

Orford Ness

ORFORD NESS

ORFORD

boat trip
to "Island"

quay

R. Alde

Orford
lighthouse

R. Butley

prohibited (AWRE)

Orford
Ness

Havergate Island

wire fence to H.W.M.

Crouch

main reach

21

21

Orford Island

12 The Narrows

R. Ore

15

N

15

18

9

11

Flood

North Weir Pt.

Shingle St.

F

toy shop in Aldeburgh High Street, however, and he does carry a range of tackle suitable for local conditions.

LOCAL CLUB.   Aldeburgh and District Angling Club. Secretary, Mr. C. Linsell, 115c High Street, Aldeburgh. The club runs a popular and very successful annual 'Open' in October in aid of the East Suffolk Blind Association. The beaches are pegged for 450 anglers, and good mixed bags can reasonably be expected at this time of the year. Entry fee is 5s, and the prizes are impressive.

ORFORDNESS.   (CHART NO. 8)
Orford 'Island' is in reality a long spit of shingle, wild and very remote, separated from the mainland for most of its length by the river Ore, which enters at North Wier Point. Access for beach anglers is from the quay at Orford, and there is a need to make prior arrangements for the boat trip down to the 'Island' and back again. This currently costs about 4s return, and departure is normally at about 8 or 9 a.m. from the quay. Arrangements can be made to go in the evening and return next morning.

The beach is becoming more popular, though the angler prepared to walk will always find somewhere to fish. To the north, the prohibited area controlled by the A.W.R.E. is bounded by a tall wire fence, and the area inside is patrolled by guard dogs.

The beach is of steeply shelving shingle, and fishing, especially at the 'Crouch' end, against the wire fence, is into deep water. Some tremendous bags of cod and whiting are taken here, one angler having caught five cod in an hour and a half which totalled 75lb, but this is, of course, exceptional. Good dabs, some thornbacks, and plenty of whiting are taken in season. When the sea is extremely rough, fishing is possible in the river from the other bank of the 'Island' and again some good catches are made. The river is a maze of creeks round the bird sanctuary of Havergate Island, and locals do extremely well in the deep water of some of them. Access to the creeks on foot is very difficult and far from straightforward, however.

Trailed boats can be launched at the quay at Orford, and there is ample parking space. The journey downriver to the Crouch takes about twenty minutes.

Tides are strong, and grip leads up to eight ounces are necessary at times. Otherwise tackle and baits are conventional. No bait is available on the 'Island'.

The ebb rushes out of the river at frightening speed, and there is an extremely dangerous sand bar at the mouth which must on no account be approached by the visitor. The foolhardy dinghy angler lucky enough to get out of the river in one piece, perhaps on the flood, would certainly be unable to get back in against the ebb, with or without motor. Leave well alone!

When landing on the 'Island' dinghy anglers will see the access point at the Crouch clearly enough, but care must be taken not to jar the boat against the submerged rocks at the edge of the narrow 'hard'. Dragging the dinghy across the shingle further downriver is a possibility provided the sea on the other side is calm enough for launching, but very few local anglers make the effort. Undoubtedly good dinghy fishing is to be had offshore, but the beach is very steep and is of a really wicked nature in anything but the calmest weather. Good advice it is that visitors should be satisfied with the beach fishing.

BOATS. Ralph Brinkley can be approached for transport, c/o 'The Jolly Sailor' Public House at Orford. Tel: Orford 243. Mr. Dick Elliott, The Stores, Orford, takes parties on occasions. Tel: Orford 219. Ralph Brinkley will also consider the hire of a dinghy for those wishing to make a trip alone, or in small numbers, but this must be by personal arrangement.

For visiting clubs, a very large boat is available for up to fifty-four people. The owner, Mr. F. Cane, has a full Board of Trade licence to carry that number of people, and he charges 4s 6d per head return, departure from Orford Quay according to arrangement with the club concerned. Sea fishing trips for smaller numbers can also be arranged. F. Cane, 'Janlyn', Springfield Road, Aldeburgh. Tel: Aldeburgh 2595.

For the visiting angler, the quickest access point for a trailed dinghy is at The Crouch, but about a mile further down river, access is possible at many points from there down to the Point. There is no freshwater or shelter on the 'Island' at all.

SHINGLE STREET. (CHART NO. 9)

South of the rivermouth of the Ore at North Wier Point lies the beach of Shingle Street, which, as well as fishing well for cod and whiting, has something of a reputation for thornbacks in the warmer months. For a great part of its length the beach is of steeply shelving shingle, with a sand and mud mixture at low water, and as the tide makes the angler will be able to fish into water considerably deeper than in many instances along this part of the coast.

As well as the three main species already mentioned, dogfish, soles and the occasional bass and seatrout are caught. The quality of the thornback fishing depends to a great extent upon the weather between March and June. Ideally, warm and calm seas will prevail, and night fishing is more productive, though not always essential. Most local anglers prefer to fish the flooding tide for thornbacks, since it is more likely that they will be on the move towards the rivers in which they breed at this time, but the ebb, until the water becomes really shallow, is always worth fishing.

Very near to the northern end of the beach and the Ore en-

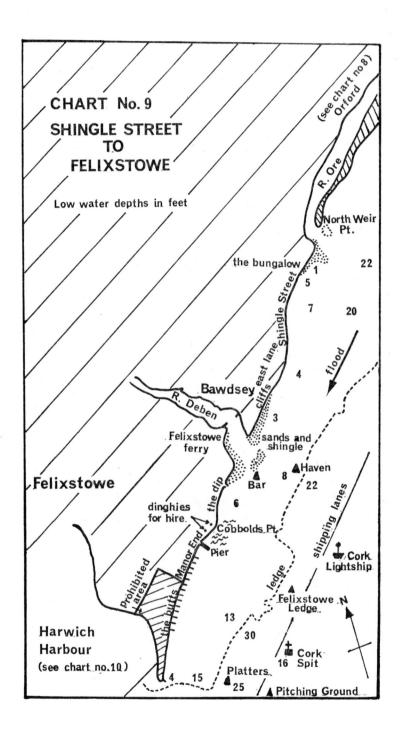

CHART No. 9

SHINGLE STREET
TO
FELIXSTOWE

Low water depths in feet

(see chart no.8)
Orford

R. Ore

North Weir Pt.

the bungalow

Shingle Street

east lane

cliffs

22

1

5

7

20

flood

4

Bawdsey

R. Deben

3

sands and shingle

Felixstowe ferry

Haven

Bar

8

22

Felixstowe

the dip

6

shipping lanes

dinghies for hire

Cobbolds Pt.

Pier

Cork Lightship

prohibited area

the butts

Manor End

ledge

Felixstowe Ledge

N

13

30

Cork Spit

16

Harwich Harbour

(see chart no.10)

4   15

Platters

25

Pitching Ground

trance is a favourite mark known as ' the bungalow ' and this is quite unmistakable, being in complete isolation, as a landmark. Many excellent bags of whiting and cod are taken. Anglers fishing into the river mouth with light tackle, allowing king rag to drift in the tide-run have picked up some useful bass, and since it is deep in places, the odd good conger is encountered by anglers fishing upriver from various points on the bank. Good bags of dabs and flounders are also encountered sometimes, but neither these nor the conger are at any time a certainty. During the early flood and the ebb, tides in the immediate vicinity of the river-mouth can be very strong, though slightly to the south the deflection of tide caused by the extensive sandbanks offshore leaves a large slack eddy which enables light tackle to be used. At this particular end of the beach the ebb tide is often more profitable than the flood, and fishing on a good night often extends to low water.

Moving south, there is plenty of fishable and productive beach, but the first Martello Tower is a noted mark for thornbacks, and fish are taken by many anglers from the stretch extending down to a second tower somewhat further south. An area of submerged wreckage is clearly visible at low water some 200 yards south of the first tower, but it claims a deal of tackle from anglers who have no opportunity to note its position before it is covered by the flood. The rest of the beach is clear of permanent snags. Rex Sheppard and Barry Cook, of Ipswich, have taken some excellent skate from this beach, best to date being one of 18lb taken by Rex in 1966.

Access to the beach is via the B1083 from Woodbridge as far as Shottisham, and then via side roads to Hollesley and on to Shingle Street. Between ' the bungalow ' and the first Martello Tower it is but a few yards from the car to the beach, but to fish further south, the angler is faced with a walk along the beach.

EAST LANE. The second Martello Tower marks what is virtually the start of East Lane, which is another excellent cod and whiting beach. Rather more care must be taken here, however, for near the remnants of wartime gun emplacements, there is thick weed offshore which can claim tackle. Before reaching this obvious mark, however, there are other hazards in the shape of clay and mudbanks offshore which also claim the leads of unwary anglers. Relatively short casts at high water will keep tackle short of these hazards, and some good pouting are taken here at times, as well as cod and whiting, plus some outstanding soles at night in October and November.

Between East Lane and the Deben entrance at Bawdsey, the beach is backed by cliffs which reach fifty feet in height. Opposite these, the water is very shallow, especially at low water, and closely spaced wooden groynes along the southern half of this stretch can be awkward to fish between in rough weather or strong tides. With so much clear and equally productive beach to the north, it is understandable that many anglers prefer the vicinity of Shingle Street. East Lane can boast some excellent catches of cod, whiting and pouting, however, and the occasional excellent bass as well.

TACKLE.   That described for other local beaches will cope well for the general run of fish here, the notable exception being that chosen for thornbacks. Reference to the notes at the beginning of the book will be useful.

BAIT.   Tackle and bait is available from the 'Anglers' Tackle Shop', 12 Market Hill, Woodbridge. Tel: Woodbridge 3573. Other sources, slightly further afield, are given at the end of the next section which deals with Felixstowe.

BOATS.   These waters can be fished by dinghy, and trailed boats can be launched at Shingle Street. It is not recommended that anglers unfamiliar with the very tricky river-mouth bring boats down from Orford Quay, and even when launching from the beach at Shingle Street, very careful note must be taken of local weather conditions. This beach is very exposed to adverse winds, and fearfully dangerous undertows, swells and surf can be the downfall of anyone attempting to get back on to the beach in bad weather. Very little extensive boat fishing is done here, but there is no doubt that cod and whiting fishing offshore, and well away from the river-mouth sandbanks, is very rewarding.

FELIXSTOWE (Suffolk). (CHART NO. 9)

Tides: −2hrs 18mins from H.W. London Bridge.

TOPOGRAPHY. The seaside town of Felixstowe lies between two estuaries. To the north the small rivermouth entrance to the Deben, with the village of Bawdsey on one bank and the hamlet of Felixstowe Ferry on the other, is a particularly hazardous one. It is flanked by sand and shingle bars which are not always clearly exposed, and which are set in a very fierce tide run. The main channel of the river is deep, but it is narrow, and lies between very steep shingle beaches until it opens into the main river.

To the south, Harwich Harbour is a busy boat terminal for inter-continental passenger traffic and all kinds of industrial shipping as well. Harwich Estuary is the outlet for the Suffolk Stour and the Orwell. Though it is a much bigger estuary than the one further north, it, too, can be hazardous. There are sand bars and 'rolling grounds' to contend with, as well as heavy boat traffic and strong tides. There is plenty of safe boat fishing to be had there, however, and this will be dealt with in due course.

SHORE FISHING. Between these estuaries there is a considerable amount of sand and shingle beach which is attractive to holiday makers as well as anglers. Happily there is very little conflict between the two interests, for summer beach fishing in this area is almost negligible as far as results are concerned. Felixstowe is essentially a winter venue for the beach angler, and the boat fishing, too, is more consistent in the colder months. Occasionally an excellent bass is taken, the most notable of which is the British record fish of 18lb 2oz which was caught by the late F. C. Borley in 1943, and which is still unbeaten. It is more than probable that serious and determined effort would produce more big bass from these beaches, but to date, most of the big ones have been taken by accident. Some seasons produce up to a dozen bass of eight pounds and over, in spite of the lack of local specialisation. (As I write, I learn that Mr. Roy Leeder of the Flag Inn, Wivenhoe, has landed a grand fish of 14lb 12½oz, fishing from his boat two miles offshore at Felixstowe!) See photograph.

During the winter months, from September onwards in fact, all the local beaches fish well for whiting and later, cod. Night fishing is generally more productive, due to the shallowness of the water and the reluctance of fish to come in too close during the daytime. Nevertheless, some very good days are enjoyed from the beaches, and it is generally well worth while fishing.

No local bait is available, but tackle dealers in Felixstowe and surrounding towns will take orders in advance for lugworm, rag, and in some cases, squid. Beach tackle suited to leads of up to eight ounces will be found suitable.

FELIXSTOWE FERRY. This small hamlet situated on the south bank of the Deben, will be of more significance to the boat angler, and will be dealt with in the boat section. A limited number of bass are taken by anglers who fish in various places around the ' point ' at the actual entrance, where there is a trace of shingle bar, but not enough for the fishing to be classed as reliable. The second Martello Tower, moving down from the Ferry, is the usual landmark quoted for the likelihood of a bass. Further south, the beach is the beginning of another more popular stretch known as ' The Dip '. Here the cod and whiting of the colder months are the main objective.

THE DIP. This beach flanks the golf course which occupies much of the land between Felixstowe itself and the Ferry. It ends more or less at Cobbold's Point, and is fishable along its length. As one nears Cobbold's Point, however, the sea bed becomes more and more rockstrewn and snag-ridden, and it is unwise to fish past the end of the line of beach huts which are set on the low cliff-side.

Access to the beach can be gained from Felixstowe Ferry, where parking can be very difficult in summer, and also at one or two points before the golf course is reached. On the extremity of Felixstowe, the road leading to Felixstowe Ferry is known as Golf Road, and just past the bomb disposal unit buildings on the left, an asphalt path leads off right, through beach hut sites, and down to the beach. Slightly nearer to the town, access on foot only may be gained by walking through a beach hut car park, but this access is not always open.

The Dip fishes well for cod and whiting from September onwards. At one time it was good for flats, but these have become increasingly rare in recent years. A few eels, flounders and the occasional bass are taken.

Prolonged easterly winds create nasty swells on this beach, and any strong wind between N.E. and S. make it difficult to fish due to heavy seas and undertow. The beach is a shallow one, and long casting can be an advantage, though it is not always essential. The beach fishes well on the rising tide, and for the first run off of the ebb.

COBBOLD'S POINT. This very short and dangerous stretch of rocky headland is easily accessible from the road running parallel to the beach near the Fludyer's Hotel. Its rocky nature means that it is virtually impossible to fish from the beach itself without losing tackle. Good bass are sometimes taken from clear spots nearby, and it is more than probable that serious fishing with expendable sinkers would, in time, produce results. No local angler has, to my knowledge, given the area an extensive trial, however. Certainly the casual visitor would be unwise to fish there for cod or whiting unless he is used to using expendable gear. There is a swirling, powerful tidal run round this headland, and when the sea is rough it is a menacing, if short stretch of beach. Bathers are warned against entering the sea in the immediate area.

FLUDYERS HOTEL TO FELIXSTOWE PIER. This stretch of beach is in Felixstowe itself, and extends parallel to much of the town's promenade. Though safe for bathing, it is quite a snaggy area, and is not fished as heavily as other beaches nearby. One or two clear spots can be found by observation at low springs, but some snags are never uncovered. Minor outcrops of rock, submerged breakwaters and old pier piles are a constant hazard, particularly in the Fludyer's Hotel area. One clear spot a little further south occurs opposite the dinghy site from which Mr. D. Goodall will hire boats to visitors for inshore fishing (see boat angling notes). This whole stretch of beach is very popular in the summer.

FELIXSTOWE PIER to MANOR END. South of the Town Pier, a long stretch of clear beach is available to the angler, almost all of it clear of permanent snags. The whole stretch fishes well for whiting and cod, especially at night, and access is very easy at many points, since the main road runs adjacent to it. The southern end, in the Butlin's area and towards the end of the promenade is perhaps more highly regarded by locals, but the whole stretch produces sport. At the extreme end of the promenade, a considerable drop occurs down to the beach, and it is unwise to fish near high water when heavy seas are running. Better to get up on the ' prom ' itself and fish from the railings.

Beyond the promenade and the beach huts, a short stretch of shingle beach occurs, before one reaches the beginning of a Ministy prohibited area known as the Butts. This is at present an army barracks, but there is a possibility that the whole area between here and Landguard Point, at the northern tip of Harwich Estuary, will be taken over for industrial development. At the moment access to the Butts is controlled by the C.O. of the barracks, but these gentlemen come and go rapidly, and anglers cannot count on being given access at all. From here down to Landguard Point then, the beach is to all intents and purposes out of reach of the angler.

FELIXSTOWE TOWN PIER.   Many years ago, this was one of the longest of our piers, and must have fished extremely well. It has since been deliberately shortened and is now only 200 yards or so in length. The present owner does have plans to extend it, however, and this will be of considerable benefit to local anglers if it comes about, and angling facilities too are extended.

The sea bed is clear of obstructions all round the pier, except directly off the end, where remains of the broken section must, by now, be festooned with gear of all kinds! Anglers can fish anywhere else in safety, however.

Like the beaches, the pier is essentially a winter one, and catches in summer are to all intents and purposes negligible. The occasional bass, a few plaice (sometimes good ones) and a few flats or eels make up catches, and few locals bother to fish it at all until the beginning of the whiting season in September, though large soles do have a habit of turning up in July and August.

The daily angling charge is currently 2s per rod, and in winter it represents, on the whole, good value. Perhaps the biggest advantage to be gained is that the pier is fishable when weather conditions are too bad for beach work. Results during easterly gales sometimes make nonsense of the idea that these winds put fish off. Unfortunately, night fishing is not allowed, except once or twice in a year by private arrangement with the owner and Felixstowe S.A.S.

The right-hand corner of the pier has something of a reputation as a ' cod corner,' and fish to 25lb have been landed. Cod are often taken from the very breakers themselves, however, and the corners aren't always the best places to make for. Grip leads are needed on all but the weakest tides, especially when the pier is thronged with anglers. Though the pier never stands dry, the water becomes very shallow from half ebb downwards, and this period of the tide is not normally productive. The pier opens at 9 a.m. and stays open until dusk. There is a tackle shop directly opposite the pier entrance.

BOAT FISHING. By any standards, the autumn whiting, and especially the cod, fishing from boats at Felixstowe is first class. Larger boats are available for hire, but this is essentially a stronghold of the dinghy angler, and the local club has a fleet of fifty or so member-owned dinghies between ten and fourteen feet kept permanently on the beach. There are ample facilities for the visiting angler to bring his own boat with him, and many people do this. There are in addition dinghies for hire from at least two places on the beach in the town itself.

The shallowness of the water inshore, and, by general standards offshore, too, is the key to the vast difference between beach and boat catches in this area. By stepping into a boat, the angler overcomes the main obstacle facing the beach angler, and cod catches in particular can be phenomenal. There is not space to go into great detail, but it is worth mentioning that as well as huge numbers of average fish, very big ones are taken as well. The present best is a 43lb fish taken by Ipswich angler Tony Marsh in March 1968, from his dinghy about two miles offshore. This is the biggest boat-caught cod taken in the British Isles, and is runner-up to the current record fish of 44½lb. Locals are confident that much bigger fish abound here, especially in late October and November, when many other heavyweight cod to over 30lb have been caught. Without being pre-occupied with big fish however, the boat angler can expect catches of fish averaging four or five pounds apiece to give total weights approaching five or six stones per rod when the fishing is at its height. Generally speaking the average weight is higher before Christmas, after which ' spring codling ' of around two pounds tend to dominate the scene.

It is fortunate that critical navigation is not necessary in order to find the fish, for many of the well-known buoys, and the Cork Lightship too, have recently been temporarily moved to different positions. Local anglers will need to re-adjust their methods of finding their favourite spots, but in general, it is not necessary to be too critical. Once one is half a mile or so offshore, whiting and cod are a near certainty once the season is well under way, and only at the beginning and end is it necessary to locate the spots known to hold the forerunners or the stragglers. Dinghy anglers and party anglers out in larger boats cover the whole area between Bawdsey and Landguard Point, and when the cod are running, they all seem to catch fish!

Perhaps the Cobbold's Point area is more consistent for cod

than any other, and with Jacob's Ladder (a white structure on stilts, set in the cliff-side just north of the Point) as a visible mark, one can fish on a general line from half to three miles out and expect to catch plenty of cod. During the season, boat fishing is so popular here that one is never alone, and the visitor should have no trouble in gaining local advice.

Most dinghy anglers use an outboard motor, since tides are strong, and rowing to the outer marks is very hard work. Since the weather is changeable, it is not in any case advisable to row offshore and risk being unable to get in against tide and wind combined. In spite of this however, it is essential to carry oars when putting to sea, for Felixstowe is no place to be without them should one's engine fail. At this stage I would refer readers to the advice given at the front of the book concerning boat fishing and seamanship. More than one foolhardy dinghy angler has drowned off this coast, and others have had narrow escapes. In emphasising how good the winter fishing can be here, I wish to counter this by pointing out that the weather can quite suddenly become very bad indeed, and risks are not worth taking.

Cobbold's Point is the most well-known general area, but the winter fishing is good down to Bawdsey and beyond. The Bawdsey area is fished by dinghy anglers pushing dinghies off from The Dip, and also from larger boats available for hire at Felixstowe Ferry. Visitors should keep well away from the river-mouth sand-bars however, for these can create bad surf when wind and tide is strong.

Summer boat angling is pleasant enough. but far less predictable than that of winter. A run of thornbacks can be expected in the spring, but is sometimes very erratic. Night fishing for this species is far more productive than day-time fishing, but adverse winds often make it inadvisable until June and later. Herring is the standard bait for thornbacks, and must be bought from fish merchants in advance. Mackerel are very infrequent visitors to Felixstowe, and cannot be in any degree expected as a possible source of fresh bait. Garfish can be taken at night at Felixstowe Ferry, and sometimes from the town pier, and these also make excellent bait for thornbacks.

An abundance of very small tope points to nearby breeding areas, but the fishing for larger fish is very uncertain. Best fish to date, and by a considerable margin, is the 47lb fish taken in 1967 by Norman Goodall, a very experienced and knowledgeable local angler. Sandy Powell has taken fish to nearly 35lb, but very few locals have taken one double-figure tope, let alone several.

Summer boat angling produces its share of unexpected results, the odd stingray, conger, brill, and lumpsucker turning up from time to time. No local, however optimistic, would expect any of these however. Dogfish are sometimes caught in numbers, but are again uncertain in their annual appearances. Plaice, dabs and flounders, together with eels and the occasional bass make up summer boat bags, and none are caught in phenomenal quantities. Like the beach fishing, Felixstowe boat angling really comes alive again with the arrival of the whiting in the autumn.

FELIXSTOWE TACKLE DEALERS. L. T. Bobby, Fishing Tackle, 57 Undercliffe Road, Felixstowe. Tel: 2709. Lug, rag and squid available if ordered in advance. Good range of tackle.

M. R. Brien, 2a Bent Hill, Felixstowe. Tel: 5318. Worms supplied when ordered in advance, good range of tackle available. Deep frozen herring and squid.

The Anglers' Tackle Shop, 12 Market Hill, Woodbridge. Tel: Woodbridge 3573. Rag and lug can be ordered, tackle supplied.

East Anglian Supplies, 37/39 Upper Orwell Street, Ipswich. Large selection of tackle available, but no bait supplied. Tel: Ipswich 51195.

BOAT HIRE. *Dinghies:* Basil Bugg, 26 St. Andrew's Road, Felixstowe. Dinghies are situated a few yards north of the pier, and can be booked in advance, a wise precaution during the winter months, especially at weekends. Current charge is £1 per boat, up to three anglers. No outboard supplied, but anglers can use their own. Approximate hours of hire 9 a.m. to 4 p.m. D. Goodall. Similar facilities available, and dinghies are kept about half a mile further north along the beach. Mr. Goodall's address is Alexander Cottages, Sea Road, Felixstowe.

PARTY ANGLING. Large boats are available for hire from the Deben entrance at Felixstowe Ferry, and also in Harwich Harbour. (See separate coverage in next chapter.)

FELIXSTOWE FERRY. Mike Grundy, Bawdsey Lodge, Bawdsey. Tel: Shottisham 340, operates an excellent boat from the Ferry full-time throughout the year. Parties of up to eight anglers are taken out at a charge of 24s per head. Departure times vary with tides, but not a great degree. Length of fishing can be pre-arranged. A typical day would last from 9 a.m. to 4 p.m. The thirty-foot boat is extremely seaworthy, and is equipped with life-saving gear, and a simple echo sounder. Bait is not supplied. Charge is £5 for one to five anglers, with 24s per head for extra men.

Doug Goodall operates a large boat from the Ferry, and parties of anglers can contact him in advance at the address given under the dinghy heading. A minimum charge of £6 per day is made, and if more than six anglers go out together, the charge is £1 per head.

Trailed dinghies. As has been mentioned earlier, there is plenty of opportunity for anglers to launch their own dinghies at

Felixstowe. Perhaps the best spot to choose is north of the pier, where the Felixstowe S.A.S. keep a large fleet of dinghies and will be able to give local advice regarding weather conditions and marks. There is a strong possibility that within months, the club will operate from a new boat compound about a mile south of the pier, and the visitor can seek advice either there or at the spot just mentioned, where Mr. Basil Bugg will have his own dinghies for hire. The telephone number of the local coastguard station is Felixstowe 2442, but the station is not permanently manned. Weather conditions and advice can be obtained from H.M. Coast-guard, Walton-on-Naze, tel: Frinton-on-Sea 5518. The G.P.O. tape recorded weather forecast for the general area can be gained ringing Colchester 8091. I cannot emphasise too strongly the need to seek, and take, local advice when using small boats off this coast.

LOCAL CLUB. Felixstowe Sea Angling Society, Hon. Secretary: P. Thain, 61 Langer Road, Felixstowe.

LOCAL ADVICE. Mr. B. Bugg, whose dinghy hirings are slightly north of the pier will give advice on prevailing conditions. For advance information concerning weather, a local forecast is available on tape for the Essex Coast (ring Colchester 8091). The club secretary or the Author will give advice on general matters, and on-the-spot help can be obtained from the local tackle dealers.

OPEN MATCHES. The club holds a very successful ' open ' Boat Festival in October, and details can be obtained from the club secretary. No boats are provided, but addresses of local boatmen can be furnished, and there is plenty of easy access from the beaches for trailed boats. An equally popular ' Open ' Beach Festival is held at about the same time of the year.

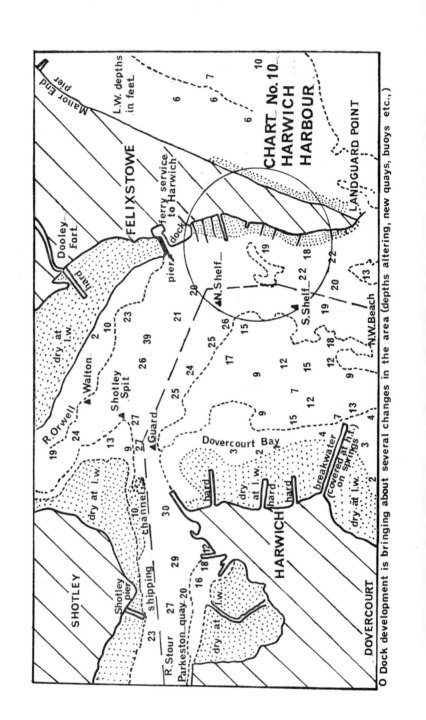

CHART No. 10
HARWICH
HARBOUR

L.W. depths in feet

Manor End pier

FELIXSTOWE

ferry service to Harwich

dock

Dooley Fort

hard

dry at l.w.

Walton

Shotley Spit

R.Orwell

Guard

SHOTLEY

Shotley pier

shipping

R.Stour
Parkeston quay

dry at l.w.

channel

dry at l.w.

Dovercourt Bay

hard

hard

dry at l.w.

HARWICH

breakwater
(covered at h.t.)

dry at l.w.

DOVERCOURT

N.Shelf

S.Shelf

N.W.Beach

LANDGUARD POINT

○ Dock development is bringing about several changes in the area (depths altering, new quays, buoys etc.,)

Essex Coast

HARWICH HARBOUR. (CHART NO. 10)

Tides as for Felixstowe.

This large and busy Suffolk/Essex estuary is viewed from two standpoints by local boat anglers. Some, like myself, consider it a useful alternative when conditions off the front at Felixstowe are too rough for my dinghy to be accommodated. Others like the harbour more than the open sea itself, and obtain all the satisfaction they ever require from boat fishing within its confines. Certainly the fishing is, at times, the equal of any in the area, and as far as thornbacks and soles are concerned it is often the best place for miles around.

ACCESS. Unfortunately for those who live on the Felixstowe side, the question of access to the harbour with a trailed dinghy is one whose anwer lies very much in the balance. The slipway which for years existed at Felixstowe Dock has been engulfed by the industrial development going on there, and the one provided as a replacement is a long way short of being satisfactory. At low tide a considerable drop occurs, about seven feet, between the top of the wall, over which a dinghy has to be negotiated, and the water surface. At high water launching and returning is not much easier due to the steepness of the sloping gravity rollers. With access through the army barracks on Landguard Point also denied to the casual visitor, the only alternative is for the boat to be taken to Dooley Fort, which is a mile or so north of Felixstowe Dock.

Access to the Dooley Fort is Ferry Road, which is a right turning from the A12 in Walton High Street, well before Felixstowe itself is reached. Turn into Maidstone Road, then follow signposts to the Dooleys Public House on the beach. Even here, however, access is possible only two hours either side of high water, due to the deep mud at the end of the ' hard '. (See Chart.)

From the Essex side, access is much more frequently obtainable and straightforward. Three launching slipways are available in Dovercourt Bay, from the road which runs along the promenade in the town of Harwich. Off Dovercourt itself a combination of marshland and a formidable sea wall in the town prevents further access to the sea.

Across the Stour at Shotley, access is again available. To the west of the pier there is a small break in the sea wall and boats can be launched at almost any state of the tide. To the east, a polite request might well result in permission to use the Ganges Naval Establishment slipway.

BOAT FISHING. As a general rule, the harbour provides very good mixed fishing, and results usually compare favourably with those 'outside'. Very few big tope are contacted, but these are not all that common in the area anyway. Some extremely big bass turn up, both unexpectedly and now and again to anglers looking for them. In winter the cod fishing leaves little to be desired, and the autumn whiting are also prolific. Spring usually sees a good run of thornbacks, which return towards the end of the summer, and the flat fishing is of a good average standard during the seasons of the various species. Soles are not, perhaps, given the attention they warrant, mainly because such small hooks and baits are required, and night fishing is almost essential for the better ones. There are literally thousands of eels in the harbour in summer and, unfortunately, an equal number of crabs!

Conger can never be ruled out, though again there are no real specialists at work. Several of up to 20lb or near have been taken from time to time, and divers working on wrecks have reported really huge fish. One or two 'unknown' quantities have been hooked, almost certainly conger.

BEACH FISHING. The scope is somewhat limited, but on the north side, the Dooley beach provides reasonable mixed fishing two hours either side of high water. Plenty of eels in summer and flounders, with the occasional bass, and a sprinkling of other species. In winter, good whiting and codling.

On the south side, Dovercourt Bay holds excellent potential for night anglers looking for soles. Fishing here is in the area used by the yacht clubs for mooring. Fishing here is possible at almost all states of the tide. Eels and flounders are also taken, and in winter the whiting and the cod are present in numbers.

PIERS AND JETTIES. Starting on the Felixstowe side, a permit is required to fish the Dock Pier, and this is obtainable from the Felixstowe Railway and Dock Company by written request. Good mixed fishing is available into deep water, with the accent, apart from flounders and eels, on autumn and winter whiting and cod.

SHOTLEY PIER is at the moment changing hands, and the future as far as angling is concerned could be exciting. There are plans for a Sea Angling Centre to be developed.

DOVERCOURT BREAKWATER ('Stone Pier'). This very low lying breakwater is full of potential, and perhaps the most notable catches in recent months have been those of big bass taken by Graham Chapman on float fished peeler crab. This young angler has an impressive list of big fish (several over 10lb, and one of 14lb!) to his credit, caught mostly, I'm sure, because he has the patience to fish, and fish, and fish! Which is about the only way of tracking down big East Coast bass. Most of the rest are taken entirely by accident. The breakwater provides good all-round fishing, entry is free at all times, but rough seas make it a very dangerous spot. There are no rails of any kind and the breakwater is not wide. It is only covered fully on the bigger tides at high water, and at low tide half of it stands dry.

BOAT FISHING. The whole aspect of boat fishing in the harbour is currently being affected by the Dock development on the Felixstowe side. New channels are being dredged, and as has already been explained, accesses are not as easy as they were. It is probable however, that some prospect will remain. It would be unwise to advise anglers that previously popular marks such as the South and North Shelf buoys are still good guides, for they may be moved, and the Shelf itself is certainly being blasted at the moment. The deep water off the Dooley is popular in the vicinity of Walton Buoy, Shotley Spit and the Guard Buoy, and fishing extends up the Stour on the Shotley side of the shipping channel, with Shotley Hole, just west of Shotley Pier, being a well-known and productive mark. Anchorage is prohibited on the opposite side of the Stour until one is well past Parkestone Quay. Thornbacks, cod, whiting, bass, etc., all run further up river, but it is the general policy of this book not to try to cover 'inland' fishing as well. Space will not allow it. Similarly, the Orwell holds very good fishing well upriver, as far as Pin Mill, with Butterman's Bay an excellent area.

Dovercourt Bay, though somewhat shallower than the areas just described, provides good mixed fishing, with soles and flats, in general, quite prolific at times. Cod and whiting also provide good sport in this area.

BOAT HIRE. A large number of big boats are available for party hire from various points round the harbour and also from villages well up the rivers Orwell and Stour. It is impossible for me to cover every boatman, but some useful names and addresses are as follows: Mr. Potts, 39a Church Street, Harwich. Tel: 2098. Mr. M. Scrutcher, 44 Kingsland, Shotley, and 'Pat' Polden, 'Celeste', Kingsland, Shotley. Tel: Shotley 282.

BAIT. Choice of bait is exactly as for other areas, and the reader will by now be familiar with this. Supplies are available from tackle shops in Felixstowe, Harwich and Dovercourt, and inland at Ipswich and Woodbridge. See list later.

A few lugworms can be dug at the Dooley Fort, Shotley and Dovercourt Bay, and almost any of the mud flats will provide small ragworm.

G

TACKLE. Conventional boat tackle will be suitable, but deep water and a very strong ebb tide makes leads up to 8oz, sometimes more, necessary for bottom fishing. The flood is somewhat more gentle, but runs quite hard at the peak of the tide. Small hooks are essential for soles.

NOTE. The harbour has a dirty bottom. TRIP YOUR ANCHOR!

WALTON-ON-THE-NAZE, Essex

TIDES: −2hr 9min H.W. London Bridge.

South of Dovercourt, the next striking feature of the coastline is the maze of creeks and gullies which surround Horsey Island, which itself lies behind the sea from Walton-on-the-Naze. There is very little beach fishing of significance here, for the creeks are virtually dry at low water, and access is not easy. Some boat fishing is carried on near Pye Sands and in Pennyhole Bay by local anglers when strong S. or S.E. winds make sea conditions difficult. Thornbacks are taken and whiting in season, but anglers generally prefer to fish out to sea if possible. A certain amount of trawling is also done in that area.

Just north of the Naze, which juts out to sea to some extent, the rocky coastline offers spasmodic bass fishing, but to reach it involves a long walk from the end of the lane leading to Walton Hall, and there is a danger of being cut off.

Beach fishing is therefore generally confined to the area south of where the cliffs fall to sea level, and is available from there back to the promenade and for some miles south.

THE NAZE. The groynes on this beach are few and far between, and no particular spots appear to be favoured. The beaches are heavily populated in the summer months, and not, in any case, too productive to the angler until the autumn and the arrival of the whiting. Thereafter the cod fishing is well up to average, with the accent, as always, on night fishing for best results.

During winter there is ample free parking, but in summer it is sometimes congested and is charged for.

Access to the Naze beach is via Walton High Street, travelling north, and continuing on to the end of the tarmac road and the car park, a distance of about a mile. Fishing is then possible, as stated, in front of the cliffs. Tides are moderate, and grip leads are used on the first of the ebb except on neaps. Lug is the favoured bait, and a certain amount is available for the digging at low tide, but quantities are limited, and the angler who leaves untidy holes on this popular beach will not be thanked for doing so. The other normal baits in use on this coast will also account for fish, but lug is by far the most popular choice.

TACKLE AND BAIT. Tackle and pre-ordered bait can be obtained from: John Metcalfe, Newgate Street, Walton-on-the-Naze and Peter Burril, Shop Parade, Kirby Cross.

WALTON PIER. As well as the beach fishing which extends from the Naze into Walton itself, the town boasts a half-mile long pier which is a noted centre for thornback fishing in season and for excellent whiting and cod catches during winter.

For the occasional visitor, day tickets to fish are available at 1s per rod, between 9 a.m. and 5 p.m., but a feature of the pier is the electronic season ticket system whereby anglers who pay a season fee of £2 are supplied with an electronic key in the shape of a card with a magnetic strip built into it. This enables the holder to get on and off the pier at any time of the day or night throughout the year, and a great number of such tickets are in circulation. Season ticket holders are limited to two rods each in view of the popularity of the pier at peak times such as winter nights when the cod are about. Fishing is permitted from both sides of the pier as well as the head, but the individual bags of up to a 100lb of cod per rod which are taken easily account for the fact that even this long pier gets crowded with anglers at times.

In the summer a train runs to the pier head, and throughout the winter there is a Bingo hall and heated amusement arcade in operation for the benefit of those members of the family who may not be too interested in fishing, or braving the conditions outside. The pier can be fished in all weathers. Liquid fuel lamps are banned.

Though Walton Pier is a boon to anglers, the summer sport in particular must be looked at in perspective. Thornbacks are most often taken by night fishing anglers who, armed with a season ticket, can quickly grab a rod on those warm and sultry nights when tides and weather make prospect good. At other times the normal species for the area may be expected to turn up from time to time, but along the whole of this coast, summer fishing, even in boats at times, is relatively unproductive. In a good cod or whiting season however, it would be unusual not to come away, even in daytime, with a fish or two, and results can on occasions be quite staggering. Take a drop net with you in spite of the fact that club members may have one available to help out.

Day tickets can be bought on the spot, and applications for season tickets should be made to the Pier Manager, Walton Pier, Walton-on-the-Naze, Essex.

The Walton Sea Angling Club, Hon. Secretary: L. G. Stroud Osbourne, 14 Columbine Gardens, Walton, has its headquarters on the pier.

FRINTON-ON-SEA. Barely a mile south of Walton lies the town of Frinton, and again there is beach fishing available of a good average standard for this coast. Leaving Walton and travel-

ling south, access to the beach is via a left turn into Connaught
Avenue, at Frinton level-crossing gates. Parking along the
esplanade to the right and left of the avenue is free off season,
but charged for in summer. A slipway access for trailed boats is
available opposite Grand Hotel, turning right from Connaught
Avenue, and beyond that a footpath at the north end of Frinton
Golf Course leads down to the beach. The whole stretch of beach
is fished until about half tide up, but fishing can be carried on
until high water and down tide again from the sea wall which
commences after a walk of about a quarter of a mile south from
the beginning of the golf course. The main beaches are very
heavily populated by holiday makers in summer, and this, combined with the possibility of extra fishing time from the sea wall
in winter when rising tides and rough seas make the beach
uncomfortable, tends to restrict angling throughout the year to
the golf course end of the beach. Tackle, species and baits are
normal for the area, and again a limited amount of lug is diggable
at low tide. Wooden groynes are often covered by rising tides on
the open beach, and if possible, it will be worth noting their
positions earlier.

BOAT FISHING, WALTON AND FRINTON. Fishing from
boats is possible either from hired craft or from trailed dinghies.
The usual warnings for east coast dinghy anglers apply, and local
advice should always be sought.

Access for trailed dinghies is at frequent intervals in Walton,
and via the slipway in front of the Grand Hotel, where the cliffs
fall away to sea level. No launching charges are made.

No dinghies are at present for hire, but larger, well equipped
and safe boats are available. Precise places of departure vary
with tides and sea conditions, and arrangements will need
to be made close to the fishing date. Current charges are around
25s per head, with a minimum charge of £6, and accommodation
for, on average, up to eight rods. Bait, refreshments and tackle
are not normally supplied by boatmen, but conventional tackle
will suit, and bait can be ordered from the places mentioned in
the beach section. Boatmen, who should be contacted at least a
month in advance for weekend fishing, and a fortnight for mid-
week dates are: Frank Bloom, 'Brents', Butchers Lane, Walton-
on-the-Naze, Essex. Mr. Bloom has several boats available, and
charges etc. must be arranged in advance, as well as place, and
time of departure. Ken Shaw, 42 The Parade, Walton-on-the-Naze,
Essex. W. Farrance, 8 Newgate Street, Walton-on-the-Naze, Essex.
G. Herbert, 20 Percival Road, Walton-on-the-Naze, Essex.

The three last named boatmen each have a twenty-five foot boat
available for about eight anglers per boat.
N.B. No large boats are available for hire during January or
February. Please send s.a.e. when making enquiries.

Before outlining boat prospects, it is necessary to point out to anglers trailing dinghies that returning at low tide can mean the job of manhandling a boat over 150 yards of beach, and that submerged and unmarked wooden groynes can be a hazard when returning at or near high water. These groynes extend about a hundred yards into the sea. Even gentle winds of around force one or two make launching in the surf difficult when they blow from E, S, or S.E. Offshore winds are coped with up to force three or so by experienced boat anglers.

SPECIES CAUGHT. Compared with Felixstowe to the north, which is the last named boat angling centre of any size, catches in this area are much more varied. The cod and whiting fishing is no better, though it is very good, but thornbacks are more consistent, big tope a real possibility, and conger and stingrays much more evident here. In addition to these species, there are good dogfish, soles, dabs, flounders, and some bass, plus the usual lesser species from time to time. Mackerel are not common inshore but are sometimes taken well out.

The usual tactics employed are the normal ones for fishing at anchor rather than on the drift, which is rarely done, and leads of up to six ounces are required, more perhaps on big springs. Tope fishermen generally operate at least three miles offshore, though fish have been taken closer in. Excellent cod and whiting fishing, together with thornbacks and stingrays in summer, can be enjoyed much closer to the shore, often no more than half a mile off, and it is seldom necessary to go out more than one and a half miles. Each boatman who takes out parties has his own private preferences, but dinghy and small boat anglers do not have to operate under critical conditions in locating marks. The sea is of uniform depth, around two or three fathoms at low water, up to one and a half or two miles out. The Medusa buoy to the north, and a line running south-west roughly parallel with the shore marks the Naze Ledge and a fall off into slightly deeper water.

BAITS. Fish strips, normally herring and mackerel, will account for stingray and conger, though neither of these species are really prolific, at least not to the extent that they can be relied upon; 50lb stingrays are taken in most years between June, July and August, and conger from 10 to 40lb also in the summer months, both often by accident rather than design. For other species baits are as normal for other areas on this coast, though cuttlefish is used for cod in exception to the general rule from centres further north.

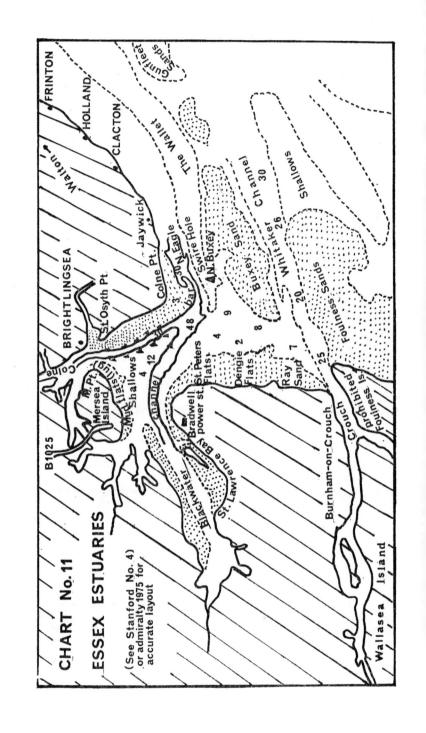

CHART No. 11

ESSEX ESTUARIES

(See Stanford No. 4)
or admiralty 1975 for
accurate layout

FRINTON
HOLLAND
CLACTON
Jaywick
Walton
BRIGHTLINGSEA
St Osyth Pt.
Colne Pt.
Colne
Mersea Island
R. Pt. (hill)
Mudflats
Shallows
channel
B1025
Bradwell
power st.
Blackwater
St. Lawrence Bay
Dengie Flats
St. Peters Flats
Ray Sand
Burnham-on-Crouch
Crouch
Foulness Is.
prohibited
Foulness
Wallasea Island
The Wallet
Gunfleet Sands
N. Eagle
Swire Hole
N. Buxey
Buxey Sand
Channel
Whitaker
Shallows
Foulness Sands
bar
N. Buxey
3
30
48
12
4
4
9
2
8
7
20
26
30
25

HOLLAND-ON-SEA

Tides (Clacton): −2hrs 5min H.W. London Bridge.

GENERAL. There are no more natural harbours south of Harwich until the Essex estuaries are reached, and offshore boat fishing is confined to dinghy work, some large boat angling, as has already been explained, from Walton-on-the-Naze, and the long trip in larger boats round from Brightlingsea etc., which will be dealt with in due course. The area does produce good fishing in winter for beach anglers however, and some of the cod fishing from dinghies is phenomenal. The area is still primarily a winter fishery, heavily populated in summer by holiday crowds, but there is little doubt that persistent fishing well offshore in suitable boats would extend the scope considerably.

BEACH FISHING—HOLLAND-ON-SEA TO CLACTON PIER. South-west from Frinton Golf Course, a long strength of beach is available in front of high cliffs. The beaches at the northern end are a little steeper than those towards the pier, and the cod fishing in particular is good. (Local angler, R. Seager, has taken fish to 22lb). The beaches are of fairly shallow sand and shingle, with small rock sometimes exposed at low water.

Access is at approximately 500 yards intervals, and parking can be a problem in summer, not so in winter. Tackle for the area is as normal on this coast, with the first of the flood and the mid-ebb requiring 5 to 6oz grips on occasions.

In addition to the cod north of Passmore Edwards, bass are occasionally taken up to 10lb between June and September, usually on ground tackle rather than special spinning gear, and flounder are present all year round. A few soles, plaice, good dabs and the occasional thornback in the period June to August complete the general prospect. Night fishing is always more productive, as it is on almost all East coast beaches. There are no snaggy areas, but care must be taken on rising tides, because these often reach the high sea wall, which runs the length of the beach.

BAIT. Some lugworm and mussel can be dug in the vicinity of the pier, best at low water. Choice of bait is as normal for the East coast, though the prospect of a summer bass makes peeler or soft crab, fresh fish baits and king ragworm a likely choice as well as the ever popular lugworm.

CLACTON PIER. The pier is a sizeable one, and the funfair and arcades are very popular with holiday makers in summer. Fishing has recently become restricted to the berthing arm at the extreme end of the pier, and here a long cast will, under favourable casting conditions, enable the angler to reach very deep water. Principal catches are, of course, the cod and whiting of the colder

months, but a fair number of thornback rays brighten prospects
for the summer angler. Good fish taken here include cod to 17½lb by
Mr. Fosker, and a wonderful bass of 15lb by Mr. R. A. Petchey.
As this book is written, a stingray of 34lb has been taken, and in
fact the British Rod-Caught record for this species, a monster of
59lb, was taken here in 1952 by Mr. J. M. Buckley. Plaice and
dabs are quite plentiful in their seasons, and some excellent bags
of flounders can be made, especially on soft or peeler crab.
Garfish appear in summer and can be taken on light tackle (see
tackle for Southend Pier). The summer months are a good time
for eels.

Tidal flow off the berthing arm is quite strong, and grip leads
up to six ounces, especially on the ebb, will be needed.

Angling fee is currently 1s per rod, and fishing is allowed
between 8 a.m. and 4.30 p.m. There is a bait shop and tackle hire
service on the pier, at the entrance to the berthing arm.

CHOICE OF BAIT is as for other local areas. Bait can be dug
(lug and mussels) under the pier at low water and on the beaches
at either side.

Access to the pier is straightforward. Parking facilities are provided at the entrance, and are free in winter, but summer parking
can be a real problem.

Clacton Sea Angling Society has an H.Q. on the pier, and the
members, particularly the officials, will be found extremely helpful
to visitors.

Clacton S.A.C., Hon. Secretary: Mike Lilley, 59 Tudor Green,
Clacton-on-Sea. Hon. Match Secretary: Peter Nunn, ' Teesdale ',
Sturricks Lane, Great Bentley, Colchester, Essex.

East coast pier fishing is, without exception, an unpredictable
business. With clear water and shallow, calm seas of summer, there
is often no real prospect of excitement. In winter things can often
be very different. Perhaps the most likely person to get the best
from this, and any other pier is the local who knows, and can
fish, when conditions are exactly right. The visitor must not be too
optimistic!

CLACTON PIER to BUTLINS HOLIDAY CAMP. The
beaches in the immediate vicinity of the pier are shallow and
generally unproductive. Though still of shallow sand, slightly
deeper water is available towards Butlins, and here the beach is
well up to average in results. A look round at low water in the
immediate vicinity of the camp will reveal a sandbar offshore, or
at least the surf created by it, and a number of old piles which
can be a hazard as far as tackle is concerned. A few peeler and
soft crab are available there, and lugworm can be dug at low
water. Another lug bed occurs further north opposite the Palace
Casino. Species, tackle and baits are as for Holland beaches.

Though very heavily populated in summer, the southern end of the beach is considered by locals to be good for cod and whiting, in winter.

BUTLINS—JAYWICK. Between Butlins and the small town of Jaywick, access to the beach by car is prohibited, but is possible from either end. Up to fifteen minutes walk along the concrete sea defence wall will be necessary after parking. The beach is of shallow sand, interspersed with rocky remnants of the old sea wall, and generally rocky at low tide. The Butlins end, being easily reached from the Clacton area is more popular with fishermen. Some good bass are taken in the summer months, again by anglers using ground tackle, and the general prospects are well up to average for the area.

A look round at low water will pinpoint any rock patches, and may provide peeler crab in season. A few lug beds exist at the Jaywick end, as well as those at Butlins already mentioned.

These beaches are becoming more popular with local anglers due to the extensive repair work and blasting going on on the sea wall at the opposite end of the town. Hitherto they were rarely fished, but are now quite heavily populated in winter, especially at night. Due to holiday crowds, the beach at either end is not a very practical proposition in summer except early or late in the day—a time when, with rising tides coinciding, the prospect of bass to 5lb is quite reasonable.

JAYWICK—LEE OVER SANDS or LEEWICK (' ST. OSYTH BEACHES '). The beaches further south-west are progressively less well explored than those nearer to Clacton. Tidal flow is strong, and access not straightforward, which probably accounts for the lack of fishing which goes on.

Access to this beach is by one route only, on foot from the car parks either in Jaywick or at the southern end of the caravan parks towards Leewick.

The beach is of gradually shelving sand, with rock and patches of mud visible at low water. The area opposite the Martello Tower is particularly rocky and punctuated by old wooden posts which are a hazard. The groynes end just south-west of the Martello Tower, and the full power of the tide is felt. Though the beaches are not fully explored, stingrays are quite frequently reported by visiting anglers who have taken them up to 20lb or so. Bass are found here, too, and some very good eels are taken in summer. A few lugworm can be dug from the area between the two groynes on the Clacton side of the Martello Tower, and some white rag is reported, though it is scarce.

LEEWICK to COLNE POINT (' POINT CLEAR '). This beach is probably even less fished than the St. Osyth beaches, because access is very difficult. One cannot reach the beach by car unless permission is obtained from the farmer who owns the only road, and this cannot be guaranteed. The beach is a shallow one, and a mixture of shingle and sand. There are no snags as far as tackle is concerned, though towards the Point there is a real danger of being cut off by rising tides. Just short of the Point there is a tidal gulley which is reputed to be good for bass, and fish to 5lb, as well as stingrays to 25lb, have been reported. Tidal flow here is very strong. A few lugworm are available at low water, together with much scarcer white ragworm. Fair bags of codling and whiting have been taken in season.

POINT CLEAR. This marks the end of beach fishing for a very long stretch of the coast. The area immediately behind the Point is a bird sanctuary, and access is prohibited.

TACKLE. Tackle for the Clacton area can be obtained from those dealers already named at Walton, or from 'Alsports', Jackson Road, Clacton-on-Sea.

BAIT. Lugworm and ragworm can be ordered in advance from: P. V. Burril, 2 and 3 The Parade, Kirby Cross, Clacton-on-Sea (also a good range of tackle).

LOCAL CLUB. Clacton Sea Angling Club. For details see Clacton Pier notes.

BOAT FISHING. There are no large boats available for hire in the Holland/Clacton area, though boats from north and south do visit the area for the excellent offshore fishing, especially in winter. The area is therefore something of a dinghy fishing strong-hold, a point evidenced by the fact the Clacton Sea Angling Club has a compound in which there are over a hundred members' dinghies.

Access to the water via a trailed dinghy is possible in at least five places. There are slipways on either side of Clacton Pier, one at Butlins and two at Holland Haven. There is no launching charge at any of them, and launching is possible at all states of the tide.

Unlike many other places on the East coast, fishing is possible in a north-east wind owing to the shelter afforded by the cliffs, but naturally the distance offshore is limited. Strong south-west, round to east winds make surf conditions very difficult on these shallow beaches.

Although the beaches are quite shallow, it is possible to reach deepish water within twenty-five minutes or so in a twelve-foot dinghy, powered by a small outboard motor. Naturally the two miles or so is not always a safe journey to consider, and Clacton is no exception from the general rule that dinghy anglers must pay attention to local weather forecasts, and seek local advice at all times.

The dinghy fishing is, of course, at its height in winter, when some truly tremendous hauls of cod, many of them big fish, are taken. The deep water of the Wallet, a huge gulley which lies between the beach and the Gunfleet Sands offshore, is the natural route for cod travelling north or south, as well as many other species. Summer fishing too can be quite good, with conger a distinct possibility and thornbacks often fishing very well indeed.

Like that in other East coast stations, Clacton's cod fishing has improved tremendously in recent years, with bags in excess of a hundredweight per rod not unknown, and individual fish of well over the thirty-pound mark included. As far as cod are concerned, my friend John Sait of Thorrington, near Brightlingsea has a history of catches which must be really hard to better. Though I have not emphasised the value of squid as a cod bait in these pages, there is no doubt that in certain years it proves deadly for cod, and John Sait was, I think, about the first angler to give it a thorough trial in our part of the world, some four or five years ago. I have a picture, which I hope will be good enough for reproduction, of John with a truly staggering catch of cod off Holland Haven. Fish of 32lb, 28lb, several of 15 to 18lb, and umpteen double-figure fish fell to his rod on one particular day, and on other occasions he has hooked enormous cod which he is quite sure were potential British records. Squid has not maintained its efficacy however, and lugworm has for the past year or two reasserted itself.

In addition to many other big cod, local anglers have accounted for a variety of specimen fish. Local Club Boat Secretary, Peter Nunn, has taken thornbacks to 21lb, Ron Stratford tope to 40lb, G. Lynch 4lb whiting (the whiting season is also extremely good here) Bob Bennett has had pouting up to 3½lb, and others, whose names I do not have, have taken conger of 32lb, stingray of 37lb, bass of 15½lb, soles up to 3lb 9½oz, etc.

Local boat anglers will point out that there are no real snags, apart from the water pipe outlet (which is buoyed) off Holland Haven about 200 yards from the shore. Local trawlermen have told me, and I have some evidence to prove it, that there are at least fifty-seven different wrecks lying in and around the Wallet off Clacton and Holland. These would not represent a hazard to anglers in small boats, apart from end tackle or anchor becoming snagged (always trip your anchor!) but they are full of potential as far as fish are concerned, particularly conger. I have been aboard a trawler which netted a piece of wreck seventeen feet by six feet by three feet and for four hours towed it inshore, since it was too heavy to winch aboard. This gives me cause to believe the trawlermen who talk of underwater snags!

A look at the Admiralty chart for the area (1975), will also reveal the reason for the lack of local ' hot spots '. One might almost say that it is all to the good! In the cod and whiting season it certainly is. Generally speaking, the depth is uniform in lines parallel to the beach, and basically the further offshore one goes, the deeper becomes the water. As East coast dinghy anglers well know however, three fathoms is plenty when it comes to catching big cod, and there is no real need to go further than a mile or so out to find these depths. A small echo sounder would undoubtedly be an asset in order to pinpoint the holes of up to six fathoms which do occur, but to all intents and purposes, and especially as far as the visitor is concerned, one place is pretty much like another.

Probably the most important local feature is that south of the pier the water remains shallow for a distance offshore, especially as far south as the Priory Spit Buoy. Further north, the area off and slightly to the north of Holland is the region which is closest to the three-fathom line. Certainly, dinghy anglers fishing any distance south of the pier and intending to come in to the beach there would be well advised to do so well before low water, due to the submerged rocks and the long pull up the beach with the boat to draw it to safety.

TACKLE. With the exception of conger, which in all honesty do not turn up with great frequency, normal boat tackle for the East coast will do. Anglers fishing in winter must be prepared to do battle with really big cod, especially before Christmas, and for these a minimum line strength of 20lb would be advisable, though there should be no need, with a reasonably pliable but powerful rod, to exceed 30lb.

BAITS. Again as normal for the East coast, with lugworm the favourite for cod, squid well worth a trial, and fish strips good for whiting.

The 'speciality' for the area, namely the stingrays, are normally caught on fish strip or king ragworm. Limpet are used in this area for both cod and whiting, and though peeler and soft crab are not all that easy to obtain locally these are excellent all round baits.

LOCAL ADVICE. Club Secretaries Mike Lilley and Peter Nunn will be pleased to give advice to the visitor, and their addresses are included in the beach notes, as are tackle dealers and bait suppliers.

BOAT HIRE. There are no large boats available, and no dinghies for hire. At weekends however, the Clacton club members launch their extensive fleet of dinghies, especially in winter, and there is often the chance of making up the number with one of these friendly anglers.

Boats can be hired at Walton (see relevant notes) and they do fish in the area just described on occasions.

ESSEX ESTUARIES. (CHART NO. 11)

The beach fishing just described is in fact the last available for a very long way south. The huge coastal inlet which has leading from it the Colne Estuary, the Blackwater and the Crouch Estuary is, for the most part, flanked by very extensive sand and mud flats which are not easily reached in many cases and which, when they are reached, provide very little prospect. The tide travels in and out so far and so fast that fishing of any kind is possible for only a very short period either side of high water. Flounders, eels and the very occasional bass are the only possibility, and the fishing is really negligible.

MERSEA POINT. One exception is the short stretch of beach fishing which is possible from Mersea Point. (See Chart No. 11). Here there is deep water well within casting distance, the beach is a steep one, and the codling and whiting is quite good. There is also the odd chance of a thornback in season, and other species are taken from time to time. Access is via the B1025 from Colchester, and just past East Mersea the road comes to an end. About a half-mile walk is then necessary from the car. Lugworm can be dug at Mersea Point, as it can in many cases along these extensive mudflats.

CREEKS AND TIDAL INLETS. The chart included here does not indicate accurately the extensive and complex system of creeks, gullies, small rivers and tidal streams which are offshoots from the main waterways. These creeks do provide good flounder, mullet and eel fishing, and lugworm can be dug in quantity at low water from many of them. Access is difficult in many instances, and the area is only thinly populated. In keeping with the general restrictions imposed through lack of space in this book, it is not possible to give any further details concerning the fishing, except to point out that for the enthusiast these species, especially mullet, have great potential.

BOAT FISHING. If the beach fishing is very limited, the boat fishing off the Essex coast is quite the reverse. A vast area of water, both in the open sea and for a distance upriver when winds are bad, is available for those who fish either from dinghies or larger craft. Before the visitor who trails his boat becomes too optimistic however, it is as well to point out that a long journey is necessary from departure points in order to fish in the open sea, and dinghy fishing is very easily curtailed by winds. The common approach to all the estuaries varies very considerably in depth, and in many places there is extremely shallow water which quickly roughens in winds which would, for larger boats, be considered only light. The dinghy angler must temper his desire to fish the more productive marks for bass and thornbacks with caution.

Quite reasonable fishing is available in the various rivers themselves however, and a visit in the cod and whiting season is well worth-while to the dinghy angler. In the warmer months it would be much easier to launch from Clacton or Holland-on-Sea, a few miles to the north, in the area which has already been dealt with.

Since the boat fishing area is a large one it will be necessary to deal with it in sections. Firstly, the prospects in each of the rivers will be noted, and offshore marks will be covered separately.

RIVER COLNE. Slightly upriver, and across Brightlingsea Creek from St. Osyth Point, the town of Brightlingsea is an excellent centre from which to base a fishing holiday. Though rod and line fishing from hired boats is not a highly developed business, there is at least one full-time boatman who caters for anglers only, and several local trawlermen are prepared to take out parties of anglers by arrangement. Fuller details will be given later.

The fishing in the River Colne itself is somewhat limited. The river is rather smaller than either of the other two in the immediate area, and though there are deep stretches, the water is for the most part too shallow to hold many fish. There are great numbers of mullet in the river during the warmer months, and bags of dabs, soles, eels, flounder and the occasional bass are taken, but neither cod nor whiting of any size travel much further up the river than Mersea Point. Sheltered fishing is available there during bad weather, but it never reaches exceptional standards.

A deep channel leads out to sea from St. Osyth Point, and dinghy anglers who anchor alongside the channel, just outside the buoys which mark it, enjoy quite good mixed fishing. Cod, whiting, thornbacks, dabs, soles and some bass are taken in their seasons. Dinghy access is available only at Brightlingsea itself however, and the further one moves along the channel, the more hazardous is the return journey if strong, or even moderate, south-west winds make the shallow water away from the channel choppy. Some excellent bass fishing is to be enjoyed by anglers who make the long trip in a dinghy from Brightlingsea to the Colne Point area. This takes about three-quarters of an hour with tide helping, and the journey is definitely not advisable in anything but settled weather. It is easy to see why bass favour the area, for surf is easily created over the extensive shallows, and there is deep water at hand for fish to retire to as the tide ebbs. Those local dinghy anglers who do fish these bass often come down on the ebb, fish the deep hole which lies off Colne Point until the flood begins to make, then fish light tackle into the choppy shallower water as the tide makes. The last of the flood is used to help the journey back to Brightlingsea, and it is considered unwise to linger over the shallows, especially as the ebb is strong and any unexpected wind combines to make seas dangerous for small boats.

King ragworm is by far the most popular bait, and many bass

of three to eight pounds are taken from the ' bar ' with one or two far in excess of that. As this book is written, I learn that Tony Gregory and two companions fished from two dinghies at night, taking fifteen bass to eight pounds, several good eels, and a 21lb stingray from the bar. Since the bass is such a slow growing fish, it is fortunate in a way that the journey by dinghy is a long and often dangerous one, and that the water is too shallow for large boats to fish. Those local anglers who appreciate their bass fishing return many of the bass they catch, and the visitor ought to do likewise.

RIVER BLACKWATER. The Blackwater river is very much more sizeable than the Colne, and offers much more substantial dinghy fishing. Most of this is carried out on the northern, and deeper, side of the river. Good cod, whiting, some thornbacks, dabs, many eels, some tope, dogfish, lots of flounders and the occasional big bass, are taken at various times of the year. In bad weather it is obviously worthwhile to consider fishing in the Blackwater and the results, particularly in winter, often justify the decision.

Two points of access, one at each end of St. Lawrence Bay, are available to the dinghy angler. Both are approached along the minor roads which leave the B1012 at Latchingdon and Snoreham. From the village of Steeple there are ample signposts leading to St. Lawrence Bay. The first available access is at Ramsey Wick, where a hard beach and a concrete ramp may be used free in winter, and on a charge of 2s 6d during the holiday season. For only a short distance upriver from this launching is water deep enough to hold many fish, and most dinghy anglers therefore fish to the right, or straight out from the access. The water here is deep, up to four fathoms at low water, and tides can be very strong. Leads of at least four ounces will normally be necessary to hold bottom using medium boat gear. The deep mud bottom is not entirely free of snags, and it is advisable to trip the anchor. Larger boats use the river, but generally speaking the dinghy angler is free to anchor at will.

Few anglers launching at Ramsey will be interested in fishing downriver towards the estuary, since much nearer access is available some three miles further along the Bradwell Quay, at the seaward end of St. Lawrence Bay. A short trip down Bradwell Creek gives immediate access to deep water, well over six fathoms in many places. Good general fishing is available in sheltered water, and this is worth bearing in mind when a planned trip to sea is prevented by weather. One particularly deep spot, ' Bradwell Hole ' has at least ten fathoms at low water, but reaching it means a fairly long trip in a dinghy into a less sheltered area off The Nass. Again, most dinghy anglers restrict their fishing to the confines of the river itself. The power station outlet of warm water is an attraction to fish of many species, and it can be located by the bubbling evident offshore from the power station itself. Here good dab fishing is to be had, and some big bass are taken on king ragworm in summer, lug in the latter part of the season. Good general fishing is in fact available for all local species, and kipper fillet is a popular bait in winter, especially for dabs.

Lugworm can be dug on the flats of St. Lawrence Bay.

RIVER CROUCH.   With a difficult area to negotiate ' outside ' the rivers, it is fortunate that the Crouch offers good dinghy fishing, especially in the autumn and winter months. Owing to the long journey from access points to the mouth of the river, small boat fishing is virtually restricted to the creeks and the river, but larger boats are available for party anglers at Burnham-on-Crouch.

In the river itself the main activity occurs during the whiting and cod season. Cod to double figures are taken at this time, and in the autumn there is a very good run of dabs to $1\frac{1}{2}$lb or so. Bass are plentiful in summer and some really good fish, well over double figures, are occasionally taken. Like the bass, mullet run up into the many side creeks, and though neither of these species are fished as thoroughly as they might be, one or two local anglers have taken good specimens. In the river mouth itself the variety is a little wider, with the occasional big tope, thornback, the odd conger and bigger cod being caught in season.

BEACH FISHING is possible at various points along the river, mainly near the various points of access. On the south side, the north edge of Wallasea Island provides about two and a half miles of fishing for cod, whiting, eels, flounders, etc. The river bank is punctuated by a series of small points, and fishing from these, deep water is reachable. Between the points there are mudflats, but at the low water mark there is a sheer drop in places into the channel. Rocks, covered with weed, exist around most of the points, and it pays, if arrival can coincide with low water, to clear away some of the trailing weed before fishing. Paternoster, running leger and float tackle can all be used according to the species sought and the state of the tide. These are strong at times, and grip leads may be necessary on springs.

The area is very little fished, especially the upper reaches of the river, but it is known that good bass, mullet some cod and whiting travel as far up as Hullbridge, and good eels and flounders are always a prospect. The whole area is one which would repay exploration, especially as far as mullet and bass are concerned.

Opposite Wallasea Island, the small town of Burnham-on-Crouch provides similar beach fishing, and there is bait supply and tackle available locally. Details later.

BOAT FISHING.   Fishing in the river mouth can be obtained

via one of the trawler skippers, based at Burnham, who make
their boats available to parties, either for rod and line fishing or
trawling. Details from the tackle shop, address is given at the end
of these notes.

Access to both sides of the river is possible with trailed boats,
and there is, as has already been explained, sheltered fishing in
deep water for a variety of common species.

On the north side, the easiest access points for dinghy anglers
are at Burnham-on-Crouch, where several ' hards ', some private,
others for public use but all in practice available to the visitor,
exist. Launching is possible at all states of the tide. (Tides at
Burnham-on-Crouch: −1hr 39mins from H.W. London Bridge.)

DINGHY HIRE. Messrs. Rice and Cole, The Seawall, Burnham-
on-Crouch, have dinghies available for hire. Current charge is £1
per day, outboard engine extra. Dinghy fishing is carried out well
down and up river from Burnham. Advice concerning the best
prospects can be obtained from D. Aldridge, tackle dealer, at 3
High Street, Burnham-on-Crouch. Generally speaking the accent
is on winter sport with whiting and cod, but there are some excellent bass to be taken in summer, and September/October usually
sees an excellent run of good dabs. Popular marks are Black Point,
opposite Bridgemarsh Island, and the whole reach from Burnham
down to the entrance of the River Roach.

TACKLE DEALER. David Aldridge (late E. Swan) 3 High
Street, Burnham-on-Crouch. Tel: 2296. A good range of
tackle, advice and bait supply is available. Lugworm, king ragworm, frozen squid, herring. Mr. Aldridge will also put enquiring
anglers in touch with local trawlermen for booking of larger boats.

BAITS. As for the area in general.

LOCAL CLUB. Burnham-on-Crouch Angling Club. Hon.
Secretary: Mr. B. Cole, c/o Rice and Cole, Seawall, Burnham-on-
Crouch.

On the south side, access is again possible for trailed dinghies
at Hullbridge and further down river at Creeksea and the vicinity
of the Wardroom Hotel and Essex Marina. Access is less direct
by car for the south side of the river however.

BAIT. Many of the creeks and mudflats in this area contain
lugworm beds, though some are in danger of being dug out.
Mersey Flats and St. Lawrence Bay do have a population of worms
at the time of writing. At Brightlingsea, Arthur Ord (see boat hire
notes) will take orders for bait in advance, and Bell's fish merchant,
Brightlingea, carries frozen herring and squid.

For other bait suppliers, see Clacton area.

H

At West Mersea, R. W. Garriock (see boat hire notes) will provide bait for party anglers if ordered in advance.

Home and Sport, 31a St. Botolph's Street, Colchester, supply lugworm in the winter months, and deep frozen baits all the year round. A recent addition includes instant deep frozen lugworm from Ireland which has a growing reputation as a substitute for live lug.

OFFSHORE FISHING, COLNE, BLACKWATER, CROUCH ESTUARY. In view of the fact that access is a long way from the open sea, and the general area not very suitable for small boats during the height of the season, i.e. cod and whiting time, the offshore fishing is really in the hands of the larger boats which cater for anglers. Details of these have been given for Brightlingsea and West Mersea. So that the party angler may have some idea of what to expect however, brief details of the offshore prospects will be given.

Firstly, it is true to say that the full potential of this area is not fully explored as yet as far as rod and line angling is concerned. There is ample need for an echo sounder on board due to the varying depths and the presence of many submerged wrecks. These are a danger to trawlers (the area is extensively trawled) and do, of course, offer good prospects for rod and line fishing. The chart gives some idea of the variation in depth, and one or two marks fished by the large boats are shown, mostly in the deeper buoyed areas. Stanford or Admiralty Charts *must* be consulted for a true idea of the complex nature of these grounds.

Catches of cod and whiting in season are very good, as is to be expected for this area. In the warmer months, thornbacks, stingrays, bass, flats, and plenty of eels are caught, though crabs are a positive menace. Summer fishing can be very quiet indeed, though prospects do improve after dark. (Arthur Ord, of Brightlingsea, does take night fishing parties when required.)

It is a little difficult for the big boats to get near to the bassy shallow water, but some very big bass do turn up well out to sea as part of the everyday events. Cod to 27lb, thornbacks to 23lb, the odd common skate to 20lb, stringrays to 30lb, bass to 12lb, and the very occasional big tope, have all been taken in this area. Tope are not really fished seriously, and there is great potential here, especially if the mackerel which sometimes arrive offshore can be located.

Normal boat gear, i.e. leads up to 8oz, lines to 25lb or so will be found suitable, though on many occasions lighter gear can be used. A good range of leads is worth having, for the quickly varying depth and tidal rate does allow constant change of tackle.

The beauty of this large estuary is that, with land on three sides of it, sheltered fishing, either in the open sea or the estuaries, is possible in almost any direction and strength of wind. The

angler who has come any distance for a day's fishing naturally
wants to get to where the outlook is bright, but in the event of
bad weather it is some consolation to know that fishing will very
rarely be entirely out of the question. It is often the case, in fact,
that the river mouths provide very good cod fishing, as well as
soles of exceptional quality, and might be chosen as a better
prospect than the open sea on occasions, regardless of the weather.
It must be emphasised, of course, that only the bigger boats have
the speed and range to make for shelter. The small boat angler
is restricted to the rivers for much of the time.

Access to the boat fishing of both the Blackwater and the Colne,
for the angler who does not have the use of his own boat, is most
easily obtained from Brightlingsea. About twenty boats of mixed
size and type seem to be available, though only one man, Arthur
Ord, operates full time for the benefit of anglers. His M.F.V.
'Caronia' is moored at Brightlingsea, and leaves there daily at
about 10 a.m. with angling parties. The charge per day is 25s,
and Mr. Ord is unique in that he does not require a minimum
booking fee for the boat. Thus the odd pair of anglers stand a
good chance of being taken out if they are the only ones who
wish to go, and no increase in the charge per head is made. At
the same time visitors must be prepared to join parties made up
on the 'hard' during the morning. 'Carona' is a fifty-foot boat,
with three-foot guard rails all round, full licence as a charter
boat, cooking facilities, toilet, etc. Tackle is available for hire,
and bait can be supplied when ordered in advance. Contact
W. Arthur Ord, M.F.V. 'Caronia,' c/o Mitchell's Boat Builders,
6 High Street, Brightlingsea. Tel: 2331.

As far as the rest of the boats are concerned, the most seaworthy are, naturally enough, the commercial fishing smacks,
whose owners will take out parties occasionally. There is little
accommodation on board, no toilet to cater for mixed parties, and
the bulwarks are very low. For the experienced angler familiar with
boats, however, they are a means of access to the offshore fishing.

Arthur Ord will pass on surplus bookings, or the following
addresses may be useful: T. Sargent, 12 Maltings Road, Brightlingsea. S. Kerridge, 48 Causton Road, Colchester, weekends only.
Colchester Oyster Fishery Company Limited. Ian MacGregor, 8
Weston Road, Brightlingsea. Tel: 2728.

WEST MERSEA. Though a long way from the offshore fishing,
and therefore faced with a very long steam out to sea, especially
against a flooding tide, one or two boats are available for hire
from time to time at West Mersea. Again, these are commercial
fishermen, who will take out parties for rod and line or trawling.
Contact: Mr. R. W. Garriock, 'Redworth,' Kingsland Road, W.
Mersea. Tel.: W. Mersea 2609.

When tides are right, West Mersea boatmen will go out on the ebb and return with the flood to save travelling time. Otherwise the Blackwater mouth is the most accessible place to fish.

A glance at the chart for this area (Admiralty 1975) will quickly reveal that the area is a very complicated one. The chart (No. 11) in this book is of necessity very much simplified. The vast shallow areas are excellent breeding grounds for many species, as is evident from the playing-card sized thornbacks, minute soles and dabs, etc., which I have seen brought up (and returned) in the trawls. Outside the Gunfleet Sands, which are obviously completely out of range of smaller boats, and which are visited only rarely by the bigger ones, the general potential is tremendous. Further north, in the vast gulley known as The Wallet, there is again the possibility of outstanding catches. This area is dealt with in the section on Clacton and Holland Haven, though the lack of big boats there means that it is still a relatively unexplored area.

As a matter of interest, the trawlers operating in this general area, i.e. out of Brightlingsea, have taken soles to 4lb, thornback to 28lb, the odd brill and turbot, haddock, and big dogfish. With deepwater and plenty of wrecks about, the possibility of conger can never be ruled out.

FIRING AREA. South of the Crouch Estuary, which has been dealt with, beach fishing remains out of the question along a considerable stretch of coastline. The vast area off Foulness Island, covering the Foulness and Maplin Sands, the beach of Foulness Island and also a certain amount of the open sea inside the shipping lanes is a prohibited area, controlled by the government and reserved for experimental firing and explosive work. Fishing of significance begins again west of Shoeburyness.

8. Thames Estuary

THAMES ESTUARY—North Side. For the purpose of this book, the final stretch of coastline to be covered, which is the north bank of the Thames Estuary, will be divided into two sections. These will be the Southend-on-Sea area, and the Canvey Island area.

SOUTHEND-ON-SEA AREA. (CHART NO. 12)

Tides: −1hr 29min from H.W. London Bridge.

GENERAL NOTES. Between Shoeburyness and Chalkwell (Chart No. 12) there are approximately seven miles of beach available for fishing. The beach is uniform in character, consisting of very shallow sand and mudflats, over which the tide makes and retreats at great speed and between very distant limits. With only minor exceptions, the fishing too is uniform, and the prospects will therefore be dealt with more concisely by regarding the stretch of coast as one area. The chart explains the approximate locations of these beaches, and from east to west they are Shoebury East, Shoebury West, Thorpe Bay, Eastern Esplanade (S.O.S.) and Westcliff-on-Sea, Chalkwell (Bell Wharf).

Between the beaches named are one or two prohibited or private stretches, amongst which are the private one mile beach at Thorpe Bay, the rifle range area just west of Shoeburyness, the Corporation Loading Pier, and the Gasworks Pier, both of which are west of Victoria Road, Southend. At the western end of the beaches, between Chalkwell Station and Bell Wharf, angling is impractical because of the vast number of slip moorings permanently installed over the sands.

BEACH FISHING. Throughout the summer months, in the daytime, beach fishing is neither encouraged nor really practical, owing to the very great concentration of holiday makers. At night in summer the general prospects are eels, flounders, the odd sole, plaice, school bass, small dogfish, pouting and, in early summer, small dabs. Some better bass, in the 5 to 6lb category, are occasionally taken from East Shoebury, and although the fishing throughout is fairly uniform the beaches to the east of the pier seem to produce the better catches of plaice and dabs in their seasons. The flounder is present all the year round.

Though there is good fishing for garfish, mackerel, scad, shad, thornbacks, some tope, etc., from either the pier of boats, very few of these species are taken by beach anglers. Mullet abound

117

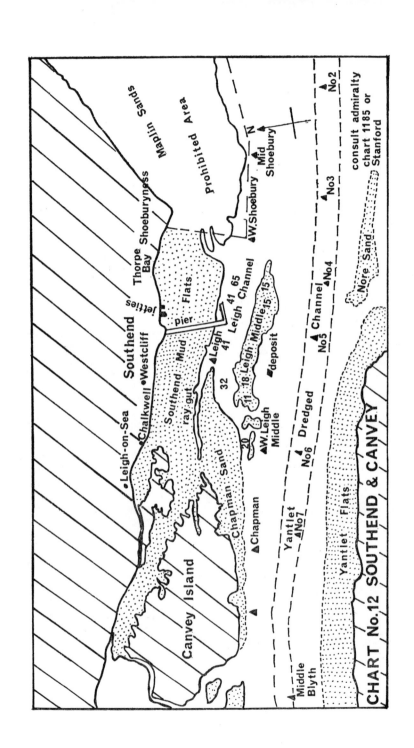

CHART No.12 SOUTHEND & CANVEY

in many of the creeks at the extreme western end of the beach, but they are not easy to catch. Anglers fishing at low water into Ray Gut take mullet and bass on float tackle in summer, and float fished peeler crab is sometimes successful, again for beach anglers at low water, from the West Knock Sands. During winter, eels and bass are replaced by codling and whiting, and the dab fishing improves.

Conventional East Coast beach tackle is used, though it can be on the lighter side. Ten to twelve-foot beach casters, lines between 15 and 22lb, and either light paternoster, running leger or Wessex leger are suitable. Grip leads are by no means essential on many occasions, and leads down to two ounces or so are frequently all that are required.

Spots which are regarded as likely to produce good all-round results are Shoebury East opposite the bathing huts, Thorpe Bay bastion, the beach east of the Gasworks Jetty, Westcliff Bathing Pool area, Westcliff Bastion, Westcliff Jetty, the Crowstone, and Bell Wharf, Chalkwell.

BAIT. Anglers almost everywhere in England are aware of the reputation which the Southend beaches have as a source of bait, particularly king ragworm. Local dealers and diggers do in fact send worms to all parts of the country, and in my own experience they arrive at their destination in good condition. The mudflats have a tremendous population of king ragworm and lug, and the angler in the area for more than just a day or two would find it well worthwhile to dig his own bait. As far as this is concerned, howevever, two points need bearing in mind. Firstly, a licence is required before one is allowed to dig, and heavy fines as well as confiscation of bait is the penalty for failing to obtain that licence. At 10s per year the charge is very reasonable, and application should be made to the Pier and Foreshore Offices, Pier Hill, Southend-on-Sea. No digging is allowed less than quarter of a mile from the high water mark. King ragworm predominate on the worm beds from April to September, after which they become scarce and lugworm dominate.

The second consideration involves tides. Since the beach is so very shallow, the low water marks of neaps and springs are widely dissimilar. The best digging is available towards low water, and during neap tides the supply of worms is much worse than during springs.

In reality therefore, only the local angler and the visitor in the area for more than a few days are likely to obtain the full benefit of collecting their own bait. The many tackle shops in the area will take orders for a wide variety of baits, provided enough notice is given by the visiting angler.

CHOICE OF BAIT. As is the case anywhere on the East coast, lugworm is the most popular all-round bait. In this area king ragworm is a good second choice, with fresh fish baits, peeler and soft crab, shrimp and sandeel also well worth trying. Sandeels can be netted at low water under the pier, using a fine nylon mesh scoop net. These are always a good speculation where bass are concerned. Eels will take almost any bait, including garden worms. Peeler crab is more extensively used in this part of the world than further north, and apart from being excellent used whole for cod and bass, parts of it will account for a wide variety of species, flounder in particular. Those anglers who successfully tempt mullet from the creeks or from the pier often do so with a ham or mutton fat paste, with bread as an ingredient. Harbour rag are also successful for these. Another local bait is peeled shrimp, often used raw for flounder and pouting, but sometimes equally successful when cooked. Like the eel, the dogfish, when it turns up in the shallow water, will take anything.

SOUTHEND PIER.   One and a third miles long, Southend Pier is reputed to be the longest in the world, and it is certainly an impressive structure. The larger part of the pier is available for fishing, and where this is not so, the areas are clearly marked. Summer anglers are often barred from sections of the pierhead due to the arrival and departure of pleasure steamers.

Though the pierhead never stands completely dry, the tide does go out for a very long way, and the one mile straight section is fishable for only about three hours either side of high water. This stretch is very popular in the summer months, and although there is room for some 400 anglers, alternate Sundays throughout the summer see many local club members supporting competitions run by the local clubs. A number of 'Open' events are held, and places are numbered and reserved for competitors until an hour after the match begins, when they are available to freelance anglers.

The pier is open to anglers from 8 a.m. until sunset throughout the year, and bona fide members of recognised angling clubs may obtain a permit to fish at night provided they send a letter of recommendation, with the application, from their own Club Secretary. During the summer when the pier illuminations are on, fishing is allowed until the last train returns at about 11 p.m.

The fishing fee is now 2s for the one and only rod allowed, and this fee includes transport by train along the pier, use of deckchairs, toilets, etc., and return by train. The trains run every few minutes throughout the day. For those who insist on walking the fishing charge is 1s 6d.

As well as the range of flats and eels to be taken from the beach, the pier offers sport in summer with mackerel, shad, scad, garfish and mullet. Sliding float tackle is used for these species as is practiced in other parts of the country, but the local method most favoured is to use a light rod of eleven or twelve feet in length with a lead at the end of a mainline of 9lb b.s., and thirty-inch snoods at intervals of three feet or so above the lead. No. 6 or 8 freshwater hooks are used on the 4 to 6lb b.s. snoods, and the tackle is swung away, underhand, rather than cast from the pier.

For these mid-water species, the baits favoured are small fish strips, very lightly nicked on to the hook point at the extreme end and allowed to stream in the tide. Shrimp pieces (boiled), herring flesh and, most successful of all for mullet, mutton or ham fat mixed with bread, are also used on this light tackle. As the book is written a 6lb 4oz mullet has been taken from the pier, and many others up to about 4lb.

Conventional ground tackle, i.e. paternoster, running leger, or French boom are used for flats, eels, etc., in summer, and for the codling, whiting, pouting which winter fishing produces.

In addition to the frequently held ' Open ' matches, the Southend Amateur Angling Society organises an annual pier angling festival in June. The two-day event run by this old established and very flourishing club is always well supported by anglers from many parts of the country, and the prize lists are very impressive. Secretaries addresses are given later.

BOAT FISHING—SOUTHEND AREA. As a glance at the charts of the area will show, there is a vast amount of water available off Southend, and in spite of the fact that there are plenty of well organised party boats operating in the hands of very good skippers, the full potential is still undiscovered.

DINGHY FISHING. At intervals along the beaches just described there are slipways provided for the launching of small boats (see chart) and these are used by dinghy anglers who fish in the very deep water of the Leigh Channel. The quickest access is probably via the long ' hard ' near the Crowstone (see chart) which enables launching into Ray Gut. As far as the dinghy angler is concerned, there is no need at all to go very far out from the low water mark. Immediately off the end of the pier there is a considerable area of water, seven-and-a-half or eight fathoms deep at low water in many places. There is excellent cod fishing to be had here in the winter months, and the whiting fishing too is well up to scratch in the autumn. Thornbacks are taken in this area from mid-April to mid-October, with a lull in July and August, and a good mark for these as well as cod and whiting is the area close to the West Shoebury Buoy.

With the very heavy Thames boat traffic always in mind, the visiting angler would be unwise to venture much further offshore than the inner limit of the Leigh Middle. Anglers who know the area well, however, and larger party craft which are less affected by the wash from huge ships do find good mixed fishing in shallower water slightly east of West Shoebury Buoy but far enough out to be very near the Yantlet dredged channel. Good fishing extends back along the ground between the outer limit of the Leigh Middle and the dredged channel.

Off Chapman Sand, in deep water between Chapman and W. Leigh Middle Buoys, several conger up to 50lb or so have been taken by boat anglers, and there is plenty of scope for this kind of fishing, still to be fully explored.

Every year in the rivers Crouch and Roach, and more often in the mid-Thames area, very big tope are taken from time to time. One of the best was that taken by Peter Littlewood of Southend in 1963. This fish weighed 64lb, and several others in the 50lb class have been encountered. As well as conventional fish baits such as fresh mackerel, small flats and live pouting, eel-tails are used by anglers who fish with big tope in mind, but these fish are more likely to be encountered by anglers fishing from the larger chartered boats.

In recent years the cod fishing all down the East coast has been extremely good, but without it, the Southend area would be hard to beat as a general mixed fishery. Flatfish in particular fish very well. Some anglers have a dislike for flounder, but dabs of excellent quality, and in the quantities found by boat anglers here, ought to satisfy anyone. Bags of up to 25lb, after gutting, and composed entirely of good sized dabs, are not unknown in a good year.

Though one or two spots have been mentioned, the whole of the area along the Leigh Middle ground out to the channel edge is available, weather permitting, to the dinghy angler, and almost all of it is likely to fulfil the visiting angler's requirements. Only the local and knowledgeable angler would contemplate fishing much further east than the West Shoebury Buoy, though charter boat skippers will obviously have a much wider range. Since the visitor will be keen to take advice from local skippers as to where prospects are best, there is little point in trying to cover, within the limitations of the space available and my own lack of intimate knowledge of the outer Thames, all the possibilities which exist. Some of those are quite exciting. As well as the more welcome tope and conger, there are stingrays, angler fish, gurnard, the occasional bream, common skate, haddock and other species which are relatively uncommon in the area. This is in fact the most likely place covered in this book to produce the unusual, or the unusually large, specimen. (I have just learned that on December 17 1968, a 47lb cod was trawled in the area—3lb over the record.)

LOCAL ADVICE.   Though there are several tackle shops in the area, and useful advice may be obtained from any of them as well as a vast range of sea fishing tackle, I could not do better than to recommend Bill Roberts as an angler helpful in the extreme, very skilful as a fisherman, and always willing to talk to anyone about fishing. He is in permanent residence behind the counter in Going's tackle shop, and his home address is 616a London Road, Westcliff-on-Sea. Bill is also Secretary and founder of the South and South-East of England Shore Casting Association, and when fishing is concluded as a topic, there is always the problem of casting a lead further than anyone else to be considered. Bill will be found equally knowledgeable and competent in that direction.

LOCAL CLUBS (Membership unrestricted). Southend Amateur Angling Society, Established 1900. Hon. Secretary: L. M. Larkins, 9 Cobham Mansions, Station Road, Westcliff-on-Sea. Leigh and Westcliff Amateur Angling Society, Established 1913. Hon, Secretary: Mr. E. Illsley, 3 Homestead Road, Hadleigh, Essex. Milton Hamlet Amateur Angling Society, Established 1921. Hon. Secretary: Mr. R. Vaughn, 160 Ashingdon Road, Rochford, Essex. Shoeburyness and Pier Head Amateur Angling Society, Established 1945. Hon. Secretary: Mr. R. A. Medhurst, 58 Tudor Gardens, Shoeburyness.

TACKLE DEALERS and BAIT SUPPLY
Going Bros, 8 High Street, Southend-on-Sea. Phone: 66439. Charlie Hoy, 'Seatac', 8 Market Place, Southend-on-Sea. Phone: 43163. F. Page, 11 Sidmouth Road, Southend-on-Sea. Phone: 47235. 'Seasports', 19 Clarence Street, Southend. Phone: 49241.
    King ragworm, lugworm and soft and peeler crab are all available in season, and must be ordered up to a month in advance when demand is high.

BOAT HIRE. Some of the boats available for hire, fully licensed and, to the best of my knowledge, thoroughly reliable, with good skippers are: John Knapp ('William Ken'), 20 Hillside Road, Leigh-on-Sea, Essex. Phone: Southend 74400. Thirty-six-foot launch, up to twelve anglers. Peter Littlewood (two boats, 'Outlaw LO7' and 'Sue Ann'). Phone: Southend 62222 (day) and 65985 (evenings). Charges approximately 2s 6d per hour per rod weekdays, 3s nights and weekends. 275 Hamstel Road, Southend. Bookings also taken at 'Fantasy Fayre', 785 Southchurch Road. D. Cooper ('Ranelagh'), 172 Elmsleigh Drive, Leigh-on-Sea. Phone: Southend 74933. J. Walker, 110 Manners Way. Phone: Southend 45345. 'Kenpat', thirty-six-foot M.F.V. £1 per rod up to twelve rods. 10 Lancaster Gardens, Southend-on-Sea. Phone: Southend 66680. Colin Knapp ('Ros Brighde'), 6 The Terrace, Church Hill, Leigh-on-Sea. Phone: Southend 74625. F. Carlin, forty-two-foot M.F.V. ('British Angler'). Flat 75, Rectory Grove, Leigh-on-Sea. Phone:

Southend 47192. 'Viking'. Ring after 7 p.m., Southend 72592.

To the best of my knowledge all these boatmen operate full-time, and are available by previous booking on any day of the week. Departure times and places (often the pierhead) by individual arrangement. Bait, and in some cases, tackle, is provided at extra cost and must be specifically ordered.

SOUTHEND-ON-SEA OPEN BOAT ANGLING FESTIVAL. This huge and very smoothly run annual event is very popular indeed, and is organised in co-operation with all the local clubs by the Pier and Foreshore Department of the Corporation of Southend-on-Sea. Entry is open to all, and the organisers take pains to put visitors in boats alongside helpful locals. The festival is usually held in mid-September, and the prize lists, both for the overall event and for the individual days, are very impressive indeed. Full details of the cost (roughly 9s for two days) and entry forms, as well as a comprehensive and extremely helpful booklet on the festival, can be obtained from, at the time of writing, Mr. G. Ward, Festival Secretary, 59 Wentworth Road, Southend-on-Sea, Essex. If any difficulty arises through change of secretary, etc., enquiries to The Manager, Pier and Foreshore Department, Civic Centre, Southend-on-Sea, are sure to be answered quickly and efficiently.

PARKING. The centre of Southend-on-Sea is a metered area, and parking is something of a problem in summer. There is a large car park in Seaway, east of the pier, and taking the first turning off the promenade. West of the pier and outside the metered area, parking is permitted on the promenade. Obviously, however, parking systems are continually being revised, and the visiting angler will, in summer, need to give himself time to adapt to local conditions before starting to fish!

CANVEY ISLAND. Moving westward from Southend, Leigh-on-Sea beaches are snag-ridden, shallow, and a very long way from the low water mark. Little fishing is carried on past Bell Wharf, though the maze of small waterways off Benfleet creek is undoubtedly the haven of plenty of good mullet. Benfleet Creek, East Haven Creek and Hole Haven Creek form a loop around Canvey Island, which offers limited fishing, and which is the southern extremity of the area covered by this book.

Access to the Island is via one road only. Leave the A13 near Hadleigh, Essex, turning right on to B1014 which crosses Benfleet Creek at South Benfleet.

Most of the fishing available is from the south coast of the Island, with a limited amount to the east. Until the sudden uplift in the general standard of cod fishing down the East coast a few years ago, there was little to be taken here apart from eels, flounder, a few bass, mullet and the odd dab or plaice, but currently the cod are making things much more interesting, possibly at the expense of the flounder stocks it seems!

The Island is heavily populated at times in the summer, but access to the beach is easy. At the most profitable time, during the winter cod season, there is ample parking space all along the sea front from Thorney Bay Camp to Sea View Jetty. At the western end there is a narrow beach, alongside shipping lanes, but near Chapman's Point to the east, as much as three-quarters of a mile separates high and low water marks. A high sea wall runs the length of the Island, shelving down at the extremities on to deep mudflats. Due to the holiday trade, fishing is prohibited by Canvey Island U.D.C. from May to September between 10 a.m. and 8 p.m. on the length of beach between Thorney Creek and Seaview Jetty.

Most of the beach is rather snaggy, but wire grip leads are not always essential, and a quick recovery of tackle avoids much loss of gear. Fishing into very deep water is possible from the methane jetties of the refinery, and permits may be obtained at the entrance gates to the refinery.

Perhaps the most productive spot for cod, and the location of several good catches of fish up to 17lb by local angler Mr. M. J. Ashby, is Scars Elbow. Night fishing in season has accounted for other good cod and a forty pounder was trawled off the Island in the Chapman Shoal area. With summer crowds, and winter cod the main prospect, night fishing is, in fact, the only serious consideration.

One most notable fish taken from Canvey in December 1967 is the 68lb 2oz new British record rod-caught angler fish, which fell to the rod of Mr. H. G. T. Legerton of Hockley, Essex, whilst he was fishing from the Concord beach, in the vicinity of the old Dutch sea wall. In all honesty it would be futile for any angler to go there fishing for ' anglers ' but this is one more example of the mystery which Father Thames still manages to hide beneath its vast surface.

TACKLE. Conventional tackle for East coast beach fishing is normal for the area, though the use of grip leads is not advised unless, on big ebbs near to the shipping lanes in places like Scars Elbow, it is essential. On other beaches four ounces of lead will be adequate. Paternosters, at least wire ones, are not much favoured by locals, the most common gear used being a sliding leger on a Clements boom, or one or more French booms adjusted as required. Nylon paternosters are a good alternative.

Fishing from the saltings at the eastern end of the Island is full of potential for mullet, which come in with the tide especially on a warm summer evening when the rising water brings them over hot soft mud to browse. Float tackle and small snad rag or mutton fat/bread paste is a good choice of bait, for this is always difficult fish.

BAIT.   There is bait to be obtained from the mudflats at low water, with lug, rag, shrimp, mussel, cockles and winkles available from the mud or the pools which punctuate it. No bait digging licence is required, but digging is forbidden less than two hundred yards from the high water mark. Good lug beds exist about a mile and a half out over the flats at the eastern end, in the direction of the West Leigh Middle Buoy. Choice of bait is as for Southend area. Peeler and soft crab is available in season from the rocks of the old Dutch sea wall west of Sea View Jetty.

TACKLE DEALERS.   Southend is about twelve miles away, and the dealers in that area are the nearest available.

LOCAL CLUB.   Canvey Island Sea Anglers Club, Hon. Secretary: Mr. A. Daniels, 4 Roodegate, Basildon, Essex. The club is essentially a travelling one, and by far the greater part of their events are held in other parts of the coast.

Index

Aldeburgh 79

Bacton 40, 45
Beeston Gap 35
Benacre 70
Blakeney 29
Brancaster 27

Caister-on-Sea 57
California 56
Canvey Island 124
Cart Gap 49
Chapel Point 15
Chapel St. Leonards 15, 18
Clacton 103
Cley 31
Cobbold's Point 88
Colne Point 105
Corton 69
Covehithe 73
Cromer 37

Dunwich 77

East Lane 85
East Runton 31, 36
Eccles 50
Essex Estuaries 109

Felixstowe 86
Frinton-on-Sea 99

Gibralter Point 15
Gorleston 62
Great Yarmouth 57

Happisburgh 47
Harwich Harbour 95
Heacham 21
Hemsby 55
Holland-on-Sea 103

Holme-next-Sea 26
Hopton 68
Horsey 53
Hunstanton 21, 26

Ingoldmells Point 15, 18

Jackson's Corner 15, 18
Jaywick 105

Kelling 33
Kessingland 70

Lee over Sands 105
Lowestoft 67

Mastins Corner 15
Mersea Point 109
Minsmere 78
Morston 29, 31
Mundesley 42

Newport 55
North Walsham 41

Orfordness 82
Ostend 47
Overstrand 41

Pakefield 69

River Blackwater 111
River Colne 110
River Crouch 112

Salthouse 33
Scolt Head 28
Scratby 56
Sea Palling 52
Sheringham 34
Shingle Street 83
Sidestrand 41

Sizewell 79
Skegness 15
Snickums, The 57
Somerton Homes 54
Southend-on-Sea 117
Southwold 75

Thornham 27
Thorpeness 79
Trimmingham 41

Walberswick 76
Walcott 46
Walton-on-the-Naze 98
Wash, The 21
Waxham 52
West Mersea 115
West Runton 35
Weybourne 33
Winterton 55
Winthorpe 15

Printed in Great Britain by
The Press at Coombelands Limited · Addlestone · Surrey